What Do You *Really* Want?

The Self's Search for Itself

Also by Thomas Galten:

Enlightenment Is Not An Ego Project
2018, River Sanctuary Publishing

What Do You *Really* Want?

The Self's Search for Itself

Thomas Karl Galten LCSW CSAC

What Do You Really Want?

Copyright © 2019 by Thomas Karl Galten

All rights reserved. No part of this book may be reproduced in any form or by any electronic or mechanical means including information storage and retrieval systems, without permission in writing from the author.

ISBN 978-1-935914-92-1

Cover and Interior design by River Sanctuary Graphic Arts

Printed in the United States of America

Additional copies available from:
www.riversanctuarypublishing.com

River Sanctuary Publishing
P.O Box 1561
Felton, CA 95018
www.riversanctuarypublishing.com
Dedicated to the awakening of the New Earth

Liberation in this life comes when one knows that God is the Doer of all things.

Ramakrishna

*When I sought God, I found only myself.
When I sought myself, I found only God.*

Awhad al-din Balyani

Acknowledgments

There are many people who have substantially influenced the writing of this book; I can specifically cite only a few of them.

For one, my good friend, David Winter. Without his painstaking collection of scores of texts and e-mails exchanged between himself and me over a period of two years, this book simply would not have come into existence. Its content follows our conversations that closely.

For another, John Hoff. We became friends through our mutual involvement with the Schlitz Audubon Nature Center in Milwaukee. We have become spiritual teachers for each other.

Thank you, also, to my friends in recovery from alcohol/drug dependency. So many of them have listened patiently as I have shared both my challenges and my joys in our fellowships of the spirit. Without them, I'd have likely never found freedom.

So too, I owe a huge thanks to such notable spiritual teachers as Mooji, Rupert Spira, Amoda Maa, Adyashanti, Eckhart Tolle, the late Alan Watts, the late Nathan Gill, John Wheeler, Leo Hartong, Jeff Foster and several others. Their work has come into my life at precisely the right moments and has greatly promoted the expansion of the Self in me.

I am also grateful to numerous counseling clients who have genuinely shared their suffering and insights with me in sessions. Their courage and willingness inspire me daily as I practice my profession.

Thanks, too, must go to my counseling and psychotherapy students whom I have had the privilege to teach at Gateway Community College in Racine and Kenosha, Wisconsin. They are often more the teachers than I am in our class sessions.

Also, I wish to thank my friend and professional colleague, Melanie Wasserman, for writing an incisive review of my first book and for encouraging me in the writing of this one. Her support has been critical.

In addition, many thanks to clinical therapists Gina Yauck, Amy Perkins, Wendy Schuster, Marie Heitkamp, Cheryl Rugg, David Drapes, Mark Hirschmann, Carin Pittelman, Caroline Schmidt, Stacey Sievert, Ivaylo Hvistov, Gerri Banks and Jan Burke. Our discussions "in the trenches" of the counseling field continue to hone my understanding. And thank you to Beth Gertsen for her passion for rock and roll oldies!

A word of thanks must also go to Carol Hubbard-Seery, professor at the University of Wisconsin-Milwaukee. Dr. Hubbard-Seery's rigorous critique of my first book, which generated several important points of clarification, served to improve the presentation of ideas in this current book.

Finally, a grateful thanks to Annie Elizaberth Porter of River Sanctuary Publishing. Her careful editing of this book, as well as my first one, made these books more coherent and readable.

All the above, of course, are manifestations of the One Self, who alone must ultimately be praised and who we each essentially are. The Self alone is the actor, thinker, and doer of all things. Absolute thanks, therefore, to the Supreme.

Contents

Preface i

Introduction vii

Phase One: The Rising Up of New Consciousness

Chapter 1. The Apparent Problem 1

Chapter 2. Egoic Identity as Addiction 8

Chapter 3. The Antidote for Addiction 10

Chapter 4. The Solution, Diversely Understood 12

Chapter 5. The Self in Search of Itself 15

Chapter 6. How Do I Awaken? 20

Chapter 7. The Breaking Through of Trans-Egoic Consciousness 33

Phase Two: Exploring the Self

Chapter 8. The Self Discovering Itself 39

Chapter 9. How to Explore the Self 43

Chapter 10. More on the Nature of the Self 47

Chapter 11. Awareness of Awareness 54

Chapter 12. What is Trans-Egoic Consciousness? 58

Chapter 13. Growing Familiarity with the Self 62

Chapter 14. "Tat Tvam Asi" – You Are That 65

Chapter 15. Consciously Being the Witness 68

Contents, cont.

Phase Three: Identifying With and As Consciousness

Chapter 16. The Expansion of the New Self 73

Chapter 17. The New Identity 77

Chapter 18. Being Who You Are 83

Chapter 19. Transpersonal Consciousness vs. Transpersonal Philosophy 86

Chapter 20. The Kingdom of Heaven 93

Chapter 21. Presence..99

Chapter 22. Spiritual Knowledge.................................101

Chapter 23. The Return of Old Consciousness 105

Chapter 24. Gratitude 111

Chapter 25. Choose Consciousness over Form.........115

Chapter 26. Before the Appearance of the Universe, I Am...119

Chapter 27. God's Self and My Self Are One and The Same 122

Chapter 28. I Am Awareness Itself...............................126

Chapter 29. Tantra: The Self Embracing Itself...........129

Chapter 30. You Are What You Are Seeking 133

Chapter 31. The Eternal Witness.................................136

Chapter 32. I Am Free..139

Conclusion 141

Bibliography..146

Preface

Spiritually speaking, the question "What do you want?" seems all too simple. Replying to it might even seem unnecessary given the obviousness of the answer. You would likely reply with: "I want spiritual (or personal) growth, as do all seekers." Or at least with something like this.

But is this what you *really* want? What, after all, is spiritual growth? Or liberation? Or realization? Or a seeker? To what do these – or any of the other words we could use and which we hear and read so frequently, especially in spiritual circles – refer? Unless we can "unpack" these terms, they remain but abstractions and our very use of them continues to convince us that we know what we want.

But do we? What do you mean by enlightenment? How will we know we have experienced it and not just become quite adept at using the term? How will our lives be different when enlightenment or liberation has arrived? Or has it arrived already? If so, do I recognize it? Or has it no need to arrive because it has always been present?

Perhaps as a psychotherapist I am somewhat more sensitive to these issues than others might be. After all, serving "on the frontlines" of the counseling profession, every day meeting with clients who present with a wide variety of concerns has inclined me to move quickly from the abstract to the experiential and to pragmatically look for any indications, however small, of the One Self's creative work in the client, the manifestations of which the client herself is often entirely unaware. In this environment, there is, I have long believed, no time for what Carl Jung called "sacrosanct unintelligibility," forays, however intellectually interesting, into speculations on causation or attempts to convince the client of the rightness of my theories on her functioning or levels of emotional distress. No psychobabble will do, either. My role, instead, is to introduce the client to the authority, and to the radical accessibility, of his own experience of awareness and thus, ultimately, to himself.

Experience is Central

Similarly, the present book is aimed at assisting the reader, not only in answering the above cited questions productively, but to then order his priorities in ways that further promote real spiritual transformation. For, as any spiritual seeker would probably acknowledge, intellectual assent or belief, on the one hand, and true heart-level knowledge, on the other, are two entirely different things.

I might, for example, as it is generally agreed among spiritual people, be able to profess, as a matter of non-dual (or "advaita," in the original Sanskrit) doctrine, that I am the One Self; to know this with conviction and certainty, however, requires direct experience of the truth. And too often an unexamined and conditioned use of terminology, no matter how earnest, can amount to an actual impediment to true realization.

This is not to claim, of course, that words and ideas are unnecessary or unimportant. But a straightforward admission that words are dualistic and relative and thus simply cannot capture reality, which is, as we will see, non-dual (or "not two," "undivided" or "of a whole") simply represents a mandate to use words as precisely as possible for the purpose of pointing effectively to reality, not to attempt a reduction of it.

My hope is that your reading of this book will augment and make more poignant whatever degree of genuine experience of awakening to your ultimate identity as the Self that is already present in you. Because if there is one thing of which we can be certain from the very start it is this: The shift from false identity to true is underway in you or you would have no interest in a book such as this one. The eternal and limitless One Self – the ground of all existence – has been for millennia seeking an expansion of awareness of itself here and there, by and through this human and that one. And once this seeking of itself has begun in a specific place and time – through you, in other words - it does not stop its search until, in this life or the next, it has found itself in pure subjectivity.

As Alan Watts has written:

> The very fact that a person begins to be interested in the spiritual life, in realization, in union with God, is a certain sign that the process of awakening has begun… [1]

The Authority of Intuitive Knowing

On the other hand, you may be skeptical of these claims. Perhaps you regard them as being without verification (though we will address the issue of verifiability later in this book). This is perfectly fine with me. I, after all, have nothing to sell anyone or convince anyone of, my objective being simply to share the perspective which I have come to know to be sustainably liberating. This book, as is true of my first one, *Enlightenment is Not an Ego Project*, is not a philosophical argument, a theological treatise or a psychological theory or hypothesis. Nor is it a spiritual "how to" or self-help book in the conventional senses of those labels. It is but a sincere effort to simply point to my and others' experience of liberation and what we have learned as a result of this unimaginable and unforeseeable phenomenon. The reader is free to take what she wants and leave the rest.

All the while, as has been stated above, emphasis in this book is placed on the reader's actual lived experience. Little appeal is made to the supposed authority of traditions ancient or modern or to sacred writings, though what truth is described in these sources remains timeless and thus can be legitimately and with integrity embraced.

Similarly, I attempt to avoid empty abstractions, however sublime such words and ideas may sound, and simply ask the reader to look within and see for yourself what you are experiencing and, in so doing, come to realize what it is you've been really wanting all along. If you take me up on my invitation, I am convinced that attention thus paid to the transformative process, which has already begun unbidden in you, will reinforce and promote it further.

More about the Use of Language and Ideas

Before we proceed, I must turn attention even more deliberately than I have done above to the issue of words and language. As was true in my first book, the following terms and phrases are entirely synonymous as each refers to the ultimate or absolute dimension: God, consciousness, awareness, pure awareness, the Self, the Supreme, the Infinite, the One, the Eternal Now, the Deep Self and the experience of awareness.

So too, as regards references to the apparent separate self (the false identity), I use several words interchangeably, including ego, ego self, the finite mind, the body/mind and the person.

It should also be noted here that all quotes from the Bible are taken from *The New Oxford Annotated Bible*, Revised Standard Version.

The Structure and Approach of this Book

Finally, this book, following the Introduction, is divided into three parts, which correspond to three phases which are discernable in the process of transformation: the "rising up" of new consciousness; the exploration of the new; and identification with and as the new.

These three phases are not original to me and are substantially parallel to the three phases of transformation discussed by several medieval mystics: purgation, illumination and union.[2] So too, the three phases of transformation should not be understood as discreet, as if movement from one phase to the next happens either in linear fashion or automatically. There is much, in other words that is discussed in Phase One that is every bit as relevant to Phases Two and Three and vice versa. Similarly, the boundaries between the phases are, to some extent, arbitrary, as is always the case whenever an attempt is made to describe, by way of developmental phases, a phenomenon that is essentially boundaryless, whole, non-linear and dynamic.

And yet, the description of the process of transformation of consciousness by way of three phases, though not the only valid means, does have merit. To highlight relevant spiritual themes which, though they cannot be separated from other related themes or viewed as necessarily following one another in time, can be better understood by distinguishing them at the relative level.

So now, in the spirit of Gautama Buddha who said, "Do not put another head above your own," let us explore further.

---

[1] Watts, Alan (1972). *The Supreme Identity: An Essay on Oriental Metaphysic and the Christian Religion*, p. 172.

[2] See the work of Dante in *Seven Story Mountain* and St. Bernard of Clairvaux in *Four Degrees of Love*. Modern authors, too, such as Evelyn Underhill, Ken Wilber, Rupert Spira and Richard Rohr have described the transformation of consciousness in phases or stages resembling, to varying degrees, the three stages I use in this book.

Introduction

The first chapter of my book, *Enlightenment is Not an Ego Project*, is entitled "What do You Want?" The chapter is essentially a brief discussion of the search for happiness, which, in that it is based upon the universal illusion of separate selfhood (or "ego-centeredness" or "ego-based consciousness") is inevitably doomed to failure as it, paradoxically, only produces more unhappiness in the earnest seeker. Just as a thirsty person who attempts to assuage his thirst by drinking salt water and only thereby becomes thirstier, what appears to promise happiness in the realm of acquisitions, possessions, relationships, activities, credentials, states of mind, sensations or sense perceptions of various types only, after a temporary relief from the desperate search, end up being insufficient. We want *more*.

Eckhart Tolle writes:

> As long as you are identified with the mind, you have an externally derived sense of self. That is to say, you get your sense of who you are from things that ultimately have nothing to do with who you are: your social role, possessions, external appearance, successes and failures, belief systems, and so on. This false, mind-made self, the ego, feels vulnerable, insecure, and is always seeking new things to identify with to give it a feeling that it exists. But nothing is ever enough to give it lasting fulfillment. Its fear remains; its sense of lack and neediness remains.[1]

If anything, the fading away of the brief respite from the restless drive only adds more urgency to the pursuit. Eventually one becomes almost entirely identified with the ego project of obtaining more – more of this, that or another. Even the refined-sounding aim to advance spiritually is, at its heart, an expression of ego's conviction that it needs more – more spiritual insights, self-transcendent moments and peak experiences. Indeed, ego attempts to co-opt spirituality in order to reinforce itself as indispensable, central and necessary to the successful search.

But ego, which is the sense of individual selfhood based upon the identification of consciousness with the body/mind, cannot – and for the sake of its own survival, must not – realize that the completion and contentment for which it is compulsively searching is already present in ample abundance *without* egoic effort in, and not beyond, the very experience of consciousness in the present moment.

How Do I Find What I am Searching For?

And yet, still we ask: "How do I get it?" This is the inevitable question asked by the mind, which is the human thinking pattern, the Self's identification with which produces the person. But, the mind, in that it is asking the questions *as mind* and thus from its limited perspective on reality, is designed only to keep ego in apparent control of the spiritual growth process, not to advance real understanding. For spiritual liberation is not effected or made possible *by* me, a separate, apparently choosing self; it is liberation *from* me, once again as I conventionally understand myself. As Shankara writes in his commentary on the Vedanta Sutras:

> Realization is shown to be of the nature of the eternally free Self....Those...who consider realization to be something to be *effected*...maintain that it depends on the action of mind, speech or body...Nor...can it be said that there is dependence on action for realization...to be obtained...for as Brahman constitutes a person's Self it is not something to be attained by that person. [Italics in the original)] [2]

In other words, if you are *already* free, you can do nothing – and need do nothing – to *become* free.

Then does liberation happen at all? If so, how? Obviously, it cannot be achieved, as achievement would imply that a separate self has obtained something which it didn't already have. And this is a strategy designed, as noted above, to reinforce the centrality of ego and thus accomplishes not freedom but a stronger identification with and as the person.

Freedom is, therefore, as Shankara notes above, of the very nature of who you are. Moreover, the freedom for which we search is *prior* to the ego/searcher and thus cannot be "found" by the searcher, who is only, it turns out, a thought among other thoughts, downstream from the Self, existing within the realm of time and space and thus illusory as an actual willing and deciding entity.

Addiction to Ego: Everyone's Addiction

As stated, the identification in humans of pure awareness with the body/mind creates the highly convincing illusion that I am a separate self, a phenomenon which has a name and a personal history, rather than the pure consciousness to which the pronoun "I" ultimately points. Indeed, pure, timeless and space less awareness plus, or mixed with, the human body/mind equals, or issues in, the sense of individual personhood. The Self by way of each human, in other words, comes to identify itself with and as the body/mind, an event that, viewed from the relative level, amounts to a cultural conditioning in which the body is understood as "containing" the indwelling and separate self. Here, then, is created, as Eckhart Tolle has put it, the "mind-made self," an illusory entity that, in addition to ego, is also often referred to as me, the person or the soul.

Further, once this illusion of separateness has been created, the pure awareness which we each ultimately are, having gotten lost in its projections, clings desperately to them believing, however unconsciously, that to lose identification as a separate self would be to fall into non-being. This is, of course, the root of the human fear of death.

A Problem with Diverse Descriptions

This overwhelming human tendency, driven by a sense of separateness, to unconsciously seek the quenching of the thirst of consciousness for itself with those things which cannot meet the need has been addressed from various cultural and linguistic angles.

The Judeo-Christian-Islamic stricture against worshipping "false gods" is but one example of a religiously-based critique of the compulsive human condition. So too, the central message of the Vedantic tradition within Hinduism (which is a principle thesis of the present book) is that the seeker is actually the one being sought – however much this is not consciously recognized – and that no lasting peace or contentment is ever found until or unless one comes to realize the truth of the statement "Tat tvam asi," which is translated into English from the original Sanskrit as "I (or You) am that." This simple declaration refers to the realization that I myself, in that I am essentially the changeless experience of being aware, am the eternal. So also, the Buddha, in identifying desire as the very root of unhappiness and suffering, taught that there can be liberation from the realm of desire and entrance into nirvana, the state of freedom or detachment from the grasping, interpreting mind.

So also, since the pioneering work of Carl Jung, the transpersonal psychology movement, which is largely a recapitulation for moderns of mystical western religion (including Gnosticism and the Sufis) and eastern esoteric wisdom, has flourished and expanded. To Jung, egoic resistance to the process of individuation (or transformation of consciousness) centrally defines the human condition and generates suffering. Influential Jungians have included Morton Kelsey, John Sanford, James Hillman, Marie-Louise Von Franz, Hans Dieckmann and Frances Vaughn.

Finally, the past 40 years or so has witnessed the arrival on the contemporary spiritual scene of non-dual (also known as "direct path") spirituality, some teachers of which include Ken Wilber, Eckhart Tolle, Jeff Foster, Mooji, Amoda Maa, Rupert Spira, Leo Hartong, Nathan Gill, John Wheeler and

Adyashanti among others. The non-dual spiritual perspective is essentially a reappearance of the Vedantic school of Hinduism cited above, founded in the 7th century by Adi Shankara, and (also as noted) its assumptions form much of the basis of the present book's message.

Description is not Prescription

But these descriptions of the human condition and subsequent liberation from it, cogent and compelling as they are, do not themselves bring the experiential and direct connection to consciousness that sets consciousness free. Nor do they imply in themselves a method of attaining freedom. They are, in other words, descriptive, not prescriptive, in that the teachings do not and cannot bring with them the actual answer to the dilemma of how to experience authentic happiness. For this, nothing less than the actual experience to which the various teachings point will suffice.

The Human Condition, Chronic and Acute

In many people, the chronic addictiveness which is the human condition becomes quite highly concentrated in specific behaviors such as the ingestion of mood-altering substances, gambling, sexual compulsivity, overeating, workaholism, codependency and the like. Counseling professionals and, indeed, the general public, have become familiar with these glaring examples of the human condition in its acute and crisis forms, which become superimposed upon the underlying and generic human condition from which they proceed.

In most of us the Self has not thus "overplayed its hand" in specific addiction. And yet, the hypnotic distraction of the human condition is possibly even more pernicious and intractable for being able to operate "under the radar" in such humans, unseen and covert. After all, if we are genuinely introspective and honest with ourselves, we might ask: Who among us has not clung to such things as social status, professional prestige, a large bank account, a beautiful or strong physique, family connections, peak spiritual experiences, intelligence or creativity, ones' spouse or partner, one's children, a political, social or religious ideology? The list, of course, could go on.

The Appearance of the Human Condition

Addiction to ego typically enters consciousness at the age of 18-24 months in all normally developed humans. What's more, addiction to ego, perfectly correlated as it is with the Self's mis-identification of itself as a person, is the central illusion which generates further illusions about the nature of other apparent selves, the world and reality in general. The human condition, like all addictions which may eventually come to follow upon it, is in the nature of a self-perpetuating, self-reinforcing cycle.

Thus is born what Ken Wilbur has called the "primary dualism," which is the deeply conditioned and unquestioned assumption that reality is fundamentally characterized by the apparent difference between me and everything which is perceived as not-me. Indeed, I am taught by others and by the language they use that I begin and end at the outer layer of the body's skin, with all form "outside" of this apparent boundary being other and that which "dwells inside" the boundary being me. This is, of course, an extraordinarily impoverished understanding of selfhood, but one which we unconsciously accept without question as it arrives at a point in human development – early childhood – during which awareness is simply unable to critically examine or reject it.

The "primary dualism," then, as it is the first illusion to grip pure awareness in humans, tends to be the last from which the Self is liberated.

Humanity's Purpose

As we further make our way through this discussion, I encourage the reader to consider how desirous seeking is related to finding. Also, to what the universal human tendency to place ultimate trust in relative and illusory things, including the separate self-sense, indicates regarding the One Self's deepest intention and how unhappiness, fully embraced and experienced without resistance, issues in the arrival of true, lasting and satisfying contentedness and peace.

For we humans are a diverse species in so many and extraordinary ways. But in what we want – which is the ultimate will of the One Self that constitutes the identity of each of us – we are all the same. As humans, we have a common purpose, since it is by and through the human species that, as we will see, the Self seeks conscious awareness of itself (what Rupert Spira calls the Self's knowing of itself knowingly). This, in turn, represents the Self's apparent return to itself, from which, of course, it has not for one moment ever really been separated, separation being merely a very convincing illusion (or, as it is sometimes put, simply the dream of the Self).

The human condition, therefore, is a problem only from the limited perspective of the mind; from the unlimited perspective of the universal timeless and space less spirit, it is God's own search for God's voluntarily estranged self, a game of divine hide-and-seek, as Alan W. Watts described it, which has been willed by the One Self from the moment of the creative Big Bang event of some 14.7 billion years ago. And it first involves, as noted in the Preface, coming to realize that living spiritual water does, in fact, flow within. Second, to partaking of that living water. And third, to identifying with and as that water.

So let us move on and look more closely at the situation in which we find ourselves.

---

[1] Tolle, Eckhart (1999). *The Power of Now: A Guide to Spiritual Enlightenment*; p. 125.

[2] Shankara. *Commentary on Vedanta Sutras*; I.i.4. Translated by G. Thibaut, in SBE, volume 34, pp. 32-33.

Phase One

The Rising Up of New Consciousness

We are witnessing in our day a relatively widespread awakening of the Self in, by and through the human form. This awakening is both the cause and the effect of the current level of crisis in the human community and in the planet's natural environment. Each of us will continue, as awareness, to realize the extraordinary implications of this awakening for the remainder of these current bodily incarnations of the Self, though the predominant tendency of the Self will continue, for the time being, to be identification with and as human body/minds.

Chapter 1

The Apparent Problem

*A*s claimed in the Preface, people who pick up a book such as this one, while doing so itself indicates that the process of awakening is underway, are nevertheless initially convinced they have a problem, or at least some questions they would like resolved. But that problem or these questions amount to more than the ordinary challenges with which we humans are faced on a daily basis.

You, the reader, therefore, might have some difficulty putting your finger on or describing your concern by way of words, ideas or language. Moreover, that with which you are struggling has decidedly not responded to your attempts at reason-based resolutions or the accomplishment of well-defined objectives. If these usual and customary methods had worked, you would not be reading this book.

You, of course, are familiar with practical life problems, as we all are, and could undoubtedly identify situations with which you have contended or are currently working to ameliorate. Some of these problems might be resolved, or at least resolvable, some partially so and others might be more ongoing or intractable.

Maybe, for instance, you have experienced the need for higher income, a better job, have had unruly or incorrigible children, been divorced or have otherwise suffered family discord, have had physical or mental health concerns or tensions with coworkers or superiors. Perhaps you live in a dangerous neighborhood, are unemployed or have no access to reliable transportation. The list, as you would likely agree, could go on.

And the one thing which each of these concerns has in common is that, however difficult they are, or have been, to resolve, there is little in them or about them that seems overwhelmingly mysterious or necessarily complex to you. If only a person(s) or a specific aspect of your life situation could be more this way or less that way. Or if only the economy would improve. Or more intelligent politicians could be elected.

Moreover, you believe, often understandably, that most of your problems are, or should be, amenable to behavioral, cognitive, relational or emotional methods or approaches, though again, you may acknowledge that your overall situation in life is partially or wholly outside of your conscious control.

But ordinary, if difficult, problems such as those we face from day to day and which are strongly correlated with our life situations are not, by and large, what drive a reader to pick up a book such as this. Indeed, practical issues are usually not what inspire people to seek psychotherapy or counseling, either. And they certainly, as a rule, tend not to drive people to seek out the spiritual dimension (though, during a crisis of whatever cause, what appear, on the surface at least, to be practical or ordinary problems can indeed provide the sense of disorientation that touches off a spiritual search).

Instead, I would suggest that what you are looking for in this book is an answer to a question which you perhaps haven't even fully formed yet. But such questions as "Why can't I find the lasting happiness which I vaguely feel that I am missing out on?" or "How am I to acquire or achieve the peace, joy and serenity that always seem to be just out of reach and which I cannot capture by any effort I make?" Or "Looked at realistically, I should be reasonably happy given my satisfactory life situation. And I do appreciate the way things are going for me. So why can't I shake this feeling that something is missing?" may come close to describing the nagging sense of discontent that you are experiencing.

This, then, I would suggest, is the dilemma: I am, as a human, apparently programmed to seek happiness. It is what I *really* want. I don't, it turns out, really want all the experiences, things, states of mind, and relationships to which I cling; instead, I want the happiness that I honestly believe these things will provide me or that happiness which I am convinced they have brought me in the past.

The plain fact that these phenomena – none of them bad, wrong or inappropriate in themselves – have failed to bring the sustained happiness which you ultimately want has perhaps not even consciously registered in you. Moreover, you have also been largely unaware of that dimension of yourself which, when known directly, does bring genuine depth-level and unchanging happiness – indeed, that dimension which *is*, in itself, the happiness you seek. Yet the drive to find that dimension, explore it and become familiar with it, continues, though, in most people, unconsciously, unrecognized and misunderstood. And that drive will persist – as it likely has through many lifetimes – until the arrival of conscious knowledge and direct experience of that limitless realm which is the true Self of all of us.

Therefore, the question "What do you really want?" is most meaningfully answered in each of us with "I seek the deepest dimension of my very Self, the 'Kingdom of Heaven', the direct experience of which is lasting, unchanging joy." For all else we may attain for the unacknowledged purpose of experiencing authentic happiness is but a substitute for this. And all substitutes lose their allure; only true realization of the Deep Self never gets old and continues to sustainably provide lasting contentment.

The Need for Liberation

What's more, spiritual freedom cannot be experienced in its fullness until the universal addiction (or "human condition") is broken, thus revealing to pure awareness its identity *both* as the awareness within which all phenomena exists *and* as all phenomena. In the course of human history and in a relatively small number of humans, the Self has thus awakened from the illusion of duality, objectivity and otherness to its identity as the awareness that is both the space within which all form exists and, at the same time, the ground, essence and central animating principle of all form. Today, say many spiritual teachers, Eckhart Tolle among them, the One Self is awakening in an unprecedented percentage of humans – with Tolle's estimate ranging in the 10-20% range.*

---

* Eckhart occasionally makes this claim in his public presentations and writings.

In the present book, I take the position, as do all teachers and writers whose message is ultimately non-dual (again, literally "not two"; lacking ultimate objectivity, boundaries or otherness), that pure awareness (or God) alone is real and that whatever exists represents what Rupert Spira has called a "modulation" of this One Self, or pure awareness, which continues simultaneously to remain the changeless witness to all phenomena. But before the full truth arrives it is our destiny – the One Self's destiny, that is – to be ensnared in and enthralled by the realm of ego and duality.

The reader has perhaps by now discerned that the search for happiness is in the nature of a self-reinforcing feedback loop driven by an assumption of lack, on the one hand, and the impossibility of satisfying this lack, on the other. As noted in the Introduction, the vicious cycle which results from this conundrum has been addressed by all the world's living religious traditions and by many noteworthy spiritual psychotherapists and philosophers, as well. "By their very seeking of it, they produce the contrary effect of losing it, for that is using the Buddha to seek for the Buddha and using mind to grasp mind…. mind and the object of its search are one," said the ancient Chinese Zen master, Huang Po.[1] From the standpoint of the human search for happiness, no truer words have ever been spoken.

Here, then, is our confounding and perplexing situation, shot through as it is with compulsion and based upon illusion. Some, as alluded to above, have even declared this, our usual unregenerate state, to be tragic in its never-ending pattern of needing, wanting and clinging. After all, as the Buddha taught, "desire" ("tanha" in the original Sanskrit) forces a search for satisfaction that, while it cannot be achieved, neither can it be escaped. Given this apparently hopeless state, despair, however cloaked with the modern cynicism and denial which today is synonymous with sophistication, seems an entirely reasonable stance. And it is from this unconscious despair that we all seek freedom through various manner of compulsive grasping.

Suffering as Inevitable and Necessary

Thus, it is that many people, perhaps relatively new to the phenomenon of the Self's awakening or with relevant teaching pertaining to it, are unable to frame their experience as creative or spiritual in nature. Instead they interpret their restlessness, discontent and suffering as indicating lack of will or perhaps a psychiatric disorder of some type. Many such persons, chronically distressed, are convinced that something is missing from their lives, though, at the same time, they may be incapable of putting a name to what they want. They have yet to consciously discover that their experience originates in, and is driven by, the search of the timeless and space less dimension – the Supreme – for its own very Self. To such persons I say: Read on. You are likely to encounter here a novel (though certainly not original to the author) understanding of your suffering.

Others, though, have indeed come to realize the truth that there is something extraordinary, even purposeful, in the urgent search for inner connection and that it, moreover, implies a dimension of the psyche with which we humans typically are unfamiliar.

If you have come to frame your experience in this way, then I believe you can be grateful indeed for the insight. For you have already come to realize what each seeker must: That what you are going through, what you are suffering, what you may feel has forced you to pick up this book and others like it is not a mental illness, a pathology or an emotional disturbance. Far from it. On the contrary, your turmoil is an unmistakable indicator that by and though you (or what you have conventionally understood to be you) the divine – the true you - is seeking conscious, fully subjective knowledge of itself.

As Roberto Assagioli has written:

> ...spiritual consciousness...before revealing itself in its positive form of enlightenment and expansion makes itself felt in a negative sense...When the process of psychospiritual transformation reaches its final and decisive stage, it sometimes produces intense suffering and an inner darkness which has been referred to by Christian mystics as the "dark night of the soul"... that "passive purification" in which... the death of [one's] old personality, or "Adam," actually takes place – a necessary condition for [one's] resurrection in Christ.[2]

Necessary indeed.

---

[1] *The Huang Po Doctrine of Universal Mind* (1947); translated by Chu Ch'an; pp.16 and 24.

[2] Assagioli, R. (1993). *Transpersonal Development: The Dimension Beyond Psychosynthesis*; pp. 112,127 and 136.

Chapter 2

EGOIC IDENTITY AS ADDICTION

Let us again, for the purpose of developing our conversation further, take up a theme first addressed in the "Introduction" – that of the essential addictiveness of the universal human condition.

Addiction, in the popular mind, is an obsession with and a compulsivity toward an identifiable substance, commodity, activity or relationship. We therefore speak of addicts and non-addicts, those who have addictions and those who do not.

Yet, addiction, as noted earlier, really afflicts all normally developed humans over the age of about two years by way of what has been called the human condition. The human condition is, as we have discussed already, essentially an addiction.

For when the One Self, through the developing human, falls into apparent separation from itself, thus creating ego (which, recall, is the identification of the Self, or I, with the body/mind), addiction to that apparent separate self is created. In other words, I become obsessed with the idea I have in my mind of myself and compulsively defend this supposed self from all perceived threats and struggle to obtain for this apparent self what I believe is necessary for its survival in a competitive world of other supposed selves all seeking the same things. Moreover, I tend inevitably to view these other apparent separate selves as either threats to me or as opportunities to exploit in some way to build myself up in my own eyes.

The human condition is, then, for all of us, the primal addiction. We are, in this sense, all addicts, as we have seen. Some of us go on to develop other, more identifiable addictions (alcohol or drugs, sex, codependence, food, gambling etc.) that are both superimposed upon the primal addiction and which exacerbate the delusions and dysfunctions of the human condition. In short, we all suffer from the universal human condition. However, some people, through the later addition of other layers of addiction, come to suffer more acutely from the human condition than do others, who continue to suffer at a more covert, even unconscious, level.

Chapter 3

THE ANTIDOTE FOR ADDICTION

Addiction, then, though most often understood as afflicting a minority of people with overwhelming obsessions and observable and specific compulsions, characterizes the human condition itself, afflicting virtually all human beings (except for children less than about two years of age and developmentally delayed persons who, in their lack of ego consciousness, cannot, by definition, be addicted to ego).

The western religious tradition has referred to this phenomenon with the term "sin" and have described it as the universal tendency toward disobedience to God's will. Moreover, western religion (mainly Judaism, Christianity and Islam) have understood the state of sin as having an ontological reality in that the uniquely human separation from God is actual, real and therefore a problem which requires divine remediation.

Eastern traditions by contrast, articulated originally within Hinduism and later finding expression in Buddhism, Zen and Taoism, teach that the human separation from God is only apparent and not ultimately real. Yes, we humans do, as pointed out above, develop ego consciousness. But ego, far from being actually and literally separate from universal and limitless consciousness (or God), is really the play (or "maya" in Sanskrit) of consciousness itself and is thus, ultimately speaking, itself a function or activity of the Godhead. In other words, God has freely chosen to lose Godself in and by the realm of form and then to play, quite convincingly, at being separate. The ultimate divine purpose, from this perspective, is for God to become, once again, fully aware of Godself *as* God (and not as "other" as it assumes itself to be in the state of maya).

What's more, it is only by way of egoic (in other words, human) consciousness that consciousness can come back together with itself, as other forms of life are not characterized by the apparent separation for which re-unification would be the solution. In short, only humans, among all of earth's many creatures, can meaningfully say "I" and believe themselves thereby to be separate selves.

Chapter 4

THE SOLUTION, DIVERSELY UNDERSTOOD

The differing ways in which the west and the east have framed the issue of the human condition has led inevitably to differing ways of framing the solution – or what I have called the antidote.

To examine this issue at length would be to roam far afield from this book's objectives. Suffice it to say that, in western terms, the very real separation between humans and God must be reconciled, as alluded to above, by way of God's gracious initiative in saving mankind from sin. The Christian answer, therefore, is redemption through and by Christ. The Jewish answer is faithfulness to the ancient covenant between the Jews and Yahweh. And the Islamic answer is obedience to the will of Allah as revealed in the Koran and by the prophet Muhammed.

The Advaitic Vedanta – and generally eastern – answer to the human condition, on the other hand, is the realization that all separation is entirely illusory. Separation between God and man, humans and other humans, humans and nature only *appears* to be real. Nothing can be separate from God as it is impossible for God – which is the ultimate reality of all forms – to be separate from God's own self.

Leo Hartong writes:

The animating energy – the One manifesting as the illusion of the many – is the source of everything, including all thoughts.[1]

It becomes clear, then, that in realizing my identity as unlimited awareness, the eternal and the infinite, I am liberated from the compulsivity and addiction of the human condition. I, as it were, transcend ego identity in the time and place known conventionally as Tom while body/mind functions continue to enable me to live in this world as an apparent human.

I perceive, from this perspective, no "other" which I might view as either threat or egoic opportunity. All beings are my very self as apparent separateness and distinctiveness are unreal. Moreover, forms of all types are understood as emanating from the one underlying Self and as having that One Self at their centers. The Self is thus the source, ground and essential identity of all form, animating all form simultaneously. In addition, that underlying Self – or God, pure consciousness, awareness, infinite or supreme – is myself. Not, of course, in my role as Tom, but in my eternal identity as the formless One Self. Tom is a character being played by the Self in the universal maya, or drama.

Further, as stated earlier, there is no need to reify awareness or the One Self as if it were a lofty and distant object that somehow needs to be approached. Indeed, the Self – or, to make this experience more immediate and real, some teachers prefer the synonymous phrase "the experience of knowing" – is present and happening right here and right now. You are it.

Conscious attention is reading these pages at this very moment. You are, in short, aware of these words (and anything else of which you are right now aware) with the same awareness that has eternally been present, unlimited and outside of both time and space. The reader, defined as a separate self, is not aware. Only awareness, which transcends the person, is aware. And you are that awareness. I alone am real in my ultimate identity as the Self. Do you need anything more than this knowledge?

---

[1] Hartong, Leo (2007). *Awakening to the Dream: The Gift of Lucid Living*; p. 59.

Chapter 5

THE SELF IN SEARCH OF ITSELF

To fully appreciate the theme of the compulsive search for happiness – that is, the human condition – and its ultimate resolution, it is necessary to consider not only the nature of the Self, but also of its ultimate purpose in the realm of objectivity and form. This chapter is thus a further exploration of consciousness specifically as it has come to a new awareness of itself by way of the human species.

For in and by humans, as noted earlier, irreducible, pure, limitless awareness – which, recall, is the only ultimate reality – has manifested what could be called a new circuit within itself. Indeed, in humans, awareness is capable of being aware of itself objectively – that is, to seemingly stand apart from itself, as it were, and reflect upon itself, to know that it knows. But this is still not the endpoint of consciousness. As Gerald Heard has written:

> ...the end of evolution is not the creation of bigger and more complicated societies and more elaborate economic structures but the attainment of a higher and more intense form of consciousness, a consciousness as much above that of the average man today as the average man's consciousness is above the animals'. [1]

What is the significance of this? What implications does this novelty have for spirituality? What really is the true nature of this apparent objectivity within the human experience? Let us address these questions.

The Arrival of Ego and the "Fall from Grace"

First, consider an example of this apparent "standing apart" from ourselves. I, Tom (and all normally developed humans over about the age of two years), know that I exist. As noted, this is not true of awareness in pre-egoic creatures; in them, awareness is unable to reflect upon itself and to know that it exists apart from the objects of awareness. Awareness in pre-egoic beings, fully absorbed as it is by that of which it is aware, is thus not aware that it is aware.

In the pre-egoic (or "pre-personal," or "pre-separate self") realm, then, there has developed no bifurcation of awareness into the "I-not I" dualism that uniquely characterizes awareness in humans. In other words, pre-egoic awareness lacks the distinction between a supposedly separate entity, "me," on the one hand, and everyone and everything else that is "not-me," on the other hand. In your cat or dog, your one-year-old child and in the tree in your front yard, though awareness is unquestionably present in these entities, there is no sense of "I," awareness having not yet become aware of either itself or an "other" by way of these beings. If there is no other, then there is no separate self and vice versa – instead, there is simply an unbroken field of awareness which is fully absorbed by and identified with the objects of which it is aware.

Moreover, the dawning of apparently objective self-awareness, or apparent separateness from the whole, represents pure awareness – having now dis-identified from all that is not the human body/mind – in the state of identification with the body/mind alone, a situation which, as we have seen, creates ego, or the apparent separate self.

Ego consciousness is thus created by the mix of pure, unlimited consciousness with the limited human body/mind. Ego, the unconscious and unquestioned assumption as to who I am – my assumption, in other words, that I am a person named Tom, with a body, a will and a history – is the illusory result of the Self identified with a human body/mind organism.

From the conventional point of view, especially expressed in western philosophy, religion and psychology (with several notable exceptions), the dawning of my sense of separateness is a sort of end point. From this perspective, still dominant worldwide, any development of awareness, mystical insight or growth in personality presupposes the existence of the separate self, with its history, demographics, name and destiny, which either achieves these things or is given them as gifts of grace.

What's more, consciousness, once it has become objectively aware of itself in the human and has subsequently dis-identified from the social and natural environment, unconsciously resists, as ego, disidentification from the body/mind. In this way, as we have seen, consciousness falls into a state of compulsive clinging to itself.

In most humans, this apparent separateness results in chronic suffering driven by the fear of annihilation and the desire for liberation, which feed each other in a self-perpetuating cycle, and which tend to manifest as a vague, often barely conscious, sense of incompleteness. This discontent, as discussed earlier, then motivates a search for wholeness by way of the usual human goals and objectives. In some of us, though, suffering reaches a state of crisis which can no longer be ignored or repressed. It is in these humans that the Self is actively awakening, and the suffering endured is, also as noted earlier, both the cause and the effect of its rising.

It is perhaps clear to the reader that, from the non-dual perspective, the arrival of ego-awareness (or "personal" consciousness) carries with it much more profound implications than it does when viewed from the traditional perspective. From the non-dual view, the coming of person-awareness is an indicator that awareness has taken a step, not merely toward realization of human individuality, but ultimately toward awareness of itself in all the Self's infiniteness and freedom. Trans-egoic consciousness, after all, must come by way of passage through egoic consciousness.

The Self's step toward realization of itself is the purpose, therefore, of the human species. Ego consciousness – and thus the human species, which is the vehicle of ego consciousness - is therefore a necessary step, but not the final step, on the One Self's journey back to itself. As Cynthia Bourgeault puts it:

> ...the very purpose of our human life is to begin to lay down...foundational building blocks of unboundaried perception. Earthly life is the womb of nondual consciousness.[2]

The way back to the Self, moreover, is often fraught with anguish, just as the prodigal son's journey back to his father (see this parable, which describes the journey of the Self, in the biblical book of St. Luke, chapter 15) was preceded and accompanied by acute suffering. The Self, after all, has, in developing egoic consciousness, left the unconscious, stable and secure connection with itself, which still characterizes the pre-egoic realm of consciousness. Such is the apparent "fall from the natural state of grace" that defines human consciousness. Restoration of the Self to itself is the next step toward fulfillment and wholeness.

---

[1] Heard, Christopher (1946). "Is Mysticism Escapism?" in *Vedanta for the Western World*; Christopher Isherwood, editor; p. 31.

[2] Bourgeault, C. (2016). *The Heart of Centering Prayer: Nondual Christianity in Theory and Practice*; p. 170.

Chapter 6

How Do I Awaken?

Having discussed, to some extent, the nature of the Self, its search for itself, and at least the incipient phase of the Self's awakening by way of the human, we will return in this chapter to the more directly experiential level of exploration which we began earlier, especially to the questions raised regarding awakening.

The complete failure, as described in both the Introduction and Chapter 1, of the usual and customary egoic methods of setting things right in the face of the crisis of powerlessness has been an entirely necessary phase in the process of transformation. For mind, also as noted earlier, cannot be de-centered by mind; this can only be accomplished by the "rising up" of the spiritual dimension, which usually is accompanied in its early stages by the experience of confusion and perplexity.

The "dark night of the soul," a particularly memorable metaphor first used by the medieval mystic St. John of the Cross, describes the process of ego's diminishment. It is only in this way that we come eventually to realize that the methods or approaches in which the world has trained us to attain happiness, paradoxically, only put real happiness further out of reach. The standard approaches are, in short, nothing but distractions.

As Rupert Spira has written:

> The mind knows nothing of happiness and love. It is precisely the dissolution of the mind that allows the ever-present but sometimes seemingly veiled happiness and love to shine, timelessly in our experience...[1]

Thus does it begin to dawn upon us that we have been searching in the world and in the mind for that which can only be accessed within (or, in other words, from the spiritual dimension). Moreover, our very efforts to lay hold of that elusive something is – based in mind as those efforts are – only blocking it and with it the true happiness which would blossom within us. It is, in other words, the desirous search of the Self for itself that obstructs its own divine light from shining in us and through us.

The situation is akin to standing in a forest looking up at a bluebird sitting directly above you in a tree. You might sincerely wish that this beautiful bird would fly down closer to you, perhaps sit next to you, even to lite on your shoulder or your outstretched hand. But any movement, including movement designed to make the bird more willing to come down to you, would only cause the bird to be less likely to do so. There is, in short, nothing you can do to attract the bird closer and, in the end, you are left to watch.

Moreover, it becomes abundantly clear that shifting the continuous and compulsive search to more appropriate or more "spiritual" objects – states of consciousness, peak experiences, more serious values and the like – is of no avail. For though many of us would readily acknowledge that these things are, at some level, more relatively satisfying than what the world has to offer, they are no more sustainable than are the more common objects and experiences to which we may have earlier in our search turned.

Consciousness needs to go deeper – to the level at which the search is driven. To the level where lie unexamined, unconscious and deeply conditioned assumptions about who we are and what we want. To the level at which we feel incomplete or in need. And then even deeper, to the level of the ground of existence itself, at which timeless, space less and formless level consciousness, finding nothing other than itself, realizes that it has all along been searching for nothing other than itself. To realize less than this is to keep in place the false necessity or unconscious compulsivity which pushes us out of the Now moment and into the mind and world, the realms of suffering. It is here that we remain apparently alienated from the One Self, which is our true Self, and from the serenity which is hidden in the eternal dimension.

As Hodgkinson puts it:

> Consciousness itself is the one, undifferentiated, ever constant, self-validating…presence…It is the witness of whatever state the intelligence undergoes…when consciousness is found to be the sole reality, the phenomenal world is known to be unreal.[2]

The Failure of the Mind's Solution Revisited

To briefly summarize our discussion to this point: A serious dilemma arises when we realize that the methods to which we have become accustomed *themselves work to prevent* the fulfillment for which we seek, thus bringing us eventually, by way of suffering, to ego's collapse. It is therefore in mind's failure, not in its success, that new life is made available as ego, mind's creation, is gradually neutralized and the light of awareness, eternally present, shines through of its own accord.

So too, as discussed above, the obstruction of ego cannot be removed through effort, however spiritual, as such effort can only amount, ironically, to a pernicious reinforcing of ego, thus adding momentum to the self-perpetuating cycle and driving the psyche further into futility.

A more poignant sense of personal powerlessness than this probably cannot be experienced as the supposed solution has been exposed as false and has, in fact, become the problem! Moreover, it appears that any form of preparation for the coming of the new is corrupted by ego's claim that it can lessen or eliminate itself.

But just as the dilemma, in all its intractability, remains, so does the necessity for direct, subjective experience as the Self, which thus seeks itself by and through this human body/mind or that, will not end its search once it has begun.

Who Seeks? Who Finds?

It stands to reason that, if ego cannot bring about the direct experience of God, then "something apparently other," pure consciousness or God's own self, must accomplish this connection. Another way of saying this is that, if the solution to the apparent problem cannot be had at the level of the problem, then it must occur at another – the ego transcendent – level.

Further, if ego thus cannot bring about liberation from ego, then liberation must occur in its own time and by its own accord. We, as apparent individuals, are wholly dependent, therefore, on what has, in religious terms, been called the grace of God. A non-religious way of saying the same thing is that freedom from the self-perpetuating cycle (sometimes called "karma") must happen entirely by itself.

Passivity vs. Surrender

"What then?" one might ask. "Am I just to sit and wait? Are you suggesting passivity? Is there really nothing I can do to be free and happy?"

In this inevitable objection raised by ego, we run again into the insoluble problem: To take purposeful steps toward the direct experience of the One Self – the mind's solution – is only to obstruct the experience as that dimension of the psyche which would be taking the steps, ego, is just that which needs to be reduced in order for the experience to shine through. And so, ego, always advocating for its own indispensability, is reinforced by the apparent efforts to be rid of it.

Yet, the opposite approach – egoic passivity – though it appears to be allowing the divine to replace ego, is just as corrupted as is the active taking of behavioral or cognitive steps toward the divine. Indeed, passivity, *for the purpose* of achieving illumination or union with the Self remains, in its focus upon its own non-effort, ego-centric nonetheless. Passivity, in other words, in that it is just as invested in the future and so every bit as ignorant of the Eternal Now as is its opposite, willed activity, serves only to tighten the cords of bondage.

All purposeful methods, then, including passivity, in that they remain at the level of the problem, eventually fail. Moreover, this failure, ironically, compels the seeker to cling even more to now experientially discredited, mind-based approaches as these are all she believes she has at her disposal.

Adyashanti has written:

> ...there's nothing "I" can do in order to surrender. Yet surrender and letting go are absolutely what is called for... In order for that to happen, it must be seen that there is no way you can do it...When you surrender the grasping at the level of the gut, it may feel like you are going to die... But you don't die; the illusion of a separate self dies...Only when you are willing to die for the sake of truth can that grasping truly and authentically let go.[3]

Moreover, in this way, the concern for such mind-based solutions as spiritual methods, practices and techniques to bring about liberation are themselves problematic in their focus on egoic effort. And yet, it is only by such experiences of unsustainability and futility that the seeker, in frank honesty, comes to acknowledge the complete inadequacy of each mind-based solution to which he has turned.

These false solutions have thus served a critically useful purpose as mind-based approaches must be ruled out – exhausted, so to speak – by way of the direct experience of their total ineffectiveness. "Mind cannot be rid of mind," as it is often put in Zen writings and teachings. But we must become deeply convinced of this and nothing convinces like the failure of all such attempts.

Putting it another way, but intending the same meaning, we could say that mind simply is unable to choose against itself or its methods as choosing is an act of the will and thus strengthens ego. But the process of trial-and-error, by which one comes to experience clearly and unequivocally the self-defeating attempts of mind to free itself, must run its course. Most of us, in other words, need to experience powerlessness directly before we will accept it and its implications.

For it is typically only by way of repeated failure that ego mind eventually collapses in the phenomenon known as surrender. Surrender is not, after all, an act of the will, a choice or a deliberate decision. Instead, surrender is a "hitting bottom" of all acts of the will designed to liberate itself. Instead of being the outcome of the will's choice, therefore, surrender is the nullification of the will as an entity conceived of as separate from the whole. God's will and my will are then ultimately seen as two ways of referring to the same phenomenon.

The process of realizing freedom is thus subtractive rather than additive, as all efforts, programs, spiritual strategies and attempts must be eliminated through their having failed, leaving in their place an openness through which the incipient experience of freedom comes spontaneously.

Many seekers, at this point, despair as it seems they have entered a sort of cul de sac, a dimension of utter hopelessness. They often reason: "If nothing to which I have clung can bring me what I really want. And if even the very act of seeking is tainted with ego. If I cannot even bring about the egoic collapse which would clear the way for the light to come on its own, then what?"

Excellent questions. And if you are asking them in one way or another, then I would encourage you to keep going, because you are intuitively understanding the point and are, as Jesus puts it in the 12th chapter of the gospel of St. Mark, "not far from the Kingdom of Heaven." The Kingdom of Heaven, that dimension of the psyche which is unknown to the mind and generally ignored by awareness in the grip of the human condition, is simply another name for what we have been unconsciously seeking – our true Self.

Indeed – to reiterate – the letting go of surrender comes about not by way of the rational mind or by an act of letting go accomplished by a separate self, but by way of the running down of mind's momentum in its honest facing of its inability to secure the lasting happiness for which it has yearned.

The Implications of Powerlessness

The above-articulated message of egoic powerlessness and divine agency and initiative strikes people in a variety of ways.

Some are disappointed, even insulted. After all, spiritual growth was supposed to be "my" project, undertaken for my betterment and the quality of my experience in the world. Certainly supported by God, yes, but ultimately up to me. Reasoning along these lines, I as Tom, Dick or Mary believe myself to be in the lead. The alternative seems only to suggest personal ineffectiveness. This response clearly exposes ego to be largely still intact.

Others respond with a degree of anxiety, as if the message that awakening is fully God's work leaves one without a rudder, steering wheel or path, a disorientation which can be highly perplexing. "You're giving me nothing to hold onto," such persons often say. "What about the tools I need to move forward spiritually?" Once again, ego remains at the center of a project.

The above two responses, in that they are based upon a desire to leave open a central place and role for ego (a desire which, of course, is itself egoic) in spiritual development, as a rule indicate that more suffering is required to further lessen egoic demand and to bring about egoic collapse and "de-commissioning."

There is, I believe, also a third response to the message that the fictional ego, person or individual self is powerless – that it has no role in spiritual awakening. Witnessed especially among people who have suffered acutely or over a long period of time, there are those who welcome the news with near immediate relief. It seems, at times, that the highest hopes of such apparent persons have been surpassed, for to them the sudden realization that "I need do nothing more!" is a huge unburdening. Consciousness at this point enters the previously mentioned Kingdom of Heaven, or or what has also been called "transpersonal" or "trans-egoic consciousness."

The ego pattern, in such cases, has reached the point of exhaustion referred to earlier and its momentum has finally run down. No longer need one look to egoic effort to either advance spiritually or to avoid spiritual disaster. All can be left to consciousness. What a weight is lifted!

This latter response also readies the spiritual transformation process to realize a further truth: If spiritual growth is God's work, and God's work alone, then perhaps the supposed self, which I have always assumed myself to be, is nothing more, as noted earlier, than a highly convincing illusion. Perhaps pure timeless, space less, unlimited and formless consciousness is really my true and actual identity.

This conclusion, of course, is not a given. Even a brief review of the history of western religion reveals, for example, that insights into egoic powerlessness have not *necessarily* evolved toward insights into the illusory nature of ego. One need only consult the work of, for examples, St. Augustine or Martin Luther to see that Christian theology has at times reached the very brink of what the Buddha called "anatta," or the "no self" perspective on reality, only to fall back into dualism.

Yet the leap from ego as entirely unable to do (or not do) anything to effect its own salvation (or liberation) to ego as entirely non-existent is not nearly as difficult as it might initially seem, though western mystics who have embraced non-duality – medieval Christians such as Meister Eckhart and John Scotus Erigena, Rabbis Gikatilla and Gerona, the American transcendentalists Emerson and Thoreau, Greek Neo-Platonists such as Plotinus, the poet William Blake and Islamic Sufis such Amin-al-din Balyani and Rumi – have often been marginalized by their respective institutional religions and cultures.

Are We Left Helpless?

But what if you believe that egoic collapse has not happened in you yet? What then? Are you doomed inevitably to more suffering? Or, to borrow a phrase from the 12 Step programs, can "the bottom be raised" so that what suffering might be required of you may be lessened?

By now the reader has seen the problems inherent in answering this question from the conventional, egoic perspective, the primary one being that to attempt a collapsing of ego is itself egoic and will only reinforce, not lessen, ego.

So too: "Watch therefore, for you know neither the day nor the hour," says Jesus in the 25th chapter of the gospel of St. Matthew. Or consider Stephen De Shazer's "Formula First Session Task," a suggestion offered by the counselor to the client toward the end of a first counseling session: "Notice between now and the next time we meet what happens in your life that you'd like to see happen more often."

The emphasis in the above citations is predicated on the truth that what one watches for, takes notice of and is aware of in the realm of the spirit will manifest. We are, in the same way, free to notice and to observe any signs or indicators in ourselves that ego is collapsing, weakening or becoming marginalized or de-centered. If we are truly ready for this liberating phenomenon, then there is no question that it will indeed appear, thus promoting the process of ego de-centering and so lessening the degree and intensity of suffering required for its accomplishment. Further, since we no longer need to identify with the compulsively seeking mind, we are free, as pure awareness, to watch, notice and witness the signs which indicate that it is slipping away. We are thus privileged to be consciously aware of the transformation which the ground of being is bringing about in us.

"So," you might respond, "the powerlessness which you describe is not the end of the story, or the 'bottom line'? There is something beyond this?"

Yes, but it cannot be "gotten." Fortunately, it also *need not* be gotten, reached or attained. Because the awareness with which you are *right now* aware – with which you are reading these words and by which you are aware of your surroundings – *is* that for which you have been searching. It is that simple. This awareness, which you have taken for granted all your life, is the omega point of the search for happiness.

What's more, this ever-present awareness is neither located in the body nor is it a function or property of the brain. Awareness pre-exists the body and all form and will continue after the body is gone. It is prior to all attempts to describe it through the mind and by way of language. It is the eternal and so, as we have seen, outside of space and time. Awareness is aware of all experiences, states of mind, perceptions, actions and events. It is aware even of the phenomenon of being aware. Indeed, awareness is the "space," one could say, within which all form occurs. It is always demonstrably right here and right now, even when the body/mind is in the state of sleep. It is who I am.

Realization of this truth of your identity comes, then, by way of grace, which brings about the weakening and death of ego and all its strategies, not by perfecting ego or improving upon its methods, but by lessening it. "He who loses his life… will find it," as Jesus says in the 10th chapter of St. Matthew.

Thus it is that egoic failure must occur. And, as noted above, we are each free to be the witness, as universal awareness, to this "death/resurrection" phenomenon right here and now without further preparation. Transformation of consciousness – or awareness subjectively aware of itself – arrives by way of a process which ego cannot understand, anticipate or appropriate, a paradoxical shift accomplished by the One Will.

Let us look more closely now at the emergence of the new Self in the wake of ego's marginalization and neutralization. As we do, you are invited to notice the changes in yourself which are the clear indicators of the coming of the kingdom of heaven in you.

---

[1] Spira, Rupert (2011). *Presence: The Art of Peace and Happiness*; p. 80.

[2] Hodgkinson, Brian (2006). *The Essence of Vedanta*; p. 79.

[3] Adyashanti (2008). *The End of Your World*; p. 152-153.

Chapter 7

THE BREAKING THROUGH OF TRANS-EGOIC CONSCIOUSNESS

As mentioned earlier, traditional eastern perspectives, such as Zen, Taoism, Buddhism and Hinduism,* acknowledge that the separate self is a necessary step of awareness along the path of enlightenment; but it is not regarded as the endpoint. According to these early non-dual perspectives, awareness must transcend and dis-identify not only from everyone and everything that is not the body/mind – it must also transcend the body/mind itself, dis-identifying from it, as well, along with the ego associated with it. The Self, or awareness, then simultaneously identifies with itself in the primal and pure subjectivity that recognizes nothing other than itself to be real and has thus arrived at the level of the trans-egoic or transpersonal (or, literally, "above and beyond" ego or the apparent person).

---

* Popular forms of these religions resemble popular forms of western religion in that they, too, tend to be based upon underlying assumptions of objectivity, separation and otherness. This similarity among world religions in their customarily practiced forms reflects the state of universal human consciousness. We are thus centrally interested in the east's spiritual insights, not necessarily in its predominant forms of piety.

It is true that, pre-awakening, one does experience a certain self-awareness and, as we have discussed, one does have the capacity as a human to "stand back" and be aware of one's awareness. And yet, prior to awakening, this human self-observation capacity (the ability to know that one exists, in other words) is misunderstood as proving the objective existence of individual separate selfhood. As transformation proceeds, the human capacity to thus reflect on oneself is revealed instead to be awareness of awareness, which brings the Self together, as it were, with itself. This is not, therefore, an awareness of myself existing as a person, but a realization that what is aware and what awareness is aware of are inseparable and that I am none other than universal, non-local unlimited awareness.

One further realizes, at this point, that the awareness that has been aware of itself as an apparent object, on the one hand, and the apparent object that I have identified myself to be and which I had apparently been objectively aware of, on the other, are the same. I had been assuming, in other words, that I can view myself as if the viewer and the viewed were two distinct realities. But it turns out, I am not two (I and myself), but one, and any objectivity in my knowing of myself has been purely an illusion. I am the one awareness. Anything of which the one awareness is aware of – whether it be an apparent separate self or anything or anyone else – are only themselves the one awareness. Since only awareness is real, how can anything be other than awareness?

Contemporary non-dual teachings, including the present book, represent, therefore, an evolution of eastern insights and western gnostic and mystical understandings, which today are expanding in all cultures worldwide and which have been reinforced and verified from the scientific perspective in the 20th century by quantum physics.

Indeed, the Self wills to realize itself, by way of the human, in the fully subjective knowledge of its ultimate identity, which is pure and unlimited awareness. Self-realization, then, represents an apparent return to the state of Self-knowledge which the Self had enjoyed prior to its becoming voluntarily involved in the realm of form.

And yet, what we are calling Self-realization is only an *apparent* return, as the Self has never *actually* been separated from itself, separation being an illusion caused by the Self's giving of itself over to, and becoming involved in, the realm of form *while simultaneously remaining*, as described earlier, the unchanging and eternal witness of all form.

Transpersonal (or trans-egoic) consciousness, therefore, does not actually "arrive," as it never was at any time absent. We thus must make allowances and concessions to the limitations inherent in language, which is inescapably dualistic. And the dualistic can neither capture nor fully describe non-dual reality; it can only point to it, as noted already in earlier chapters of this book.

Moreover, people often describe realization of the Self - which is generally a sudden event – by way of spatial metaphors (i.e. "Deep within me I have begun to feel or sense a presence that never changes." Or "I feel deep down something I've not been aware of before."). Ken Wilber, quoting R.M. Bucke, has written:

All at once I found myself wrapped in a flame-colored cloud. For an instant, I thought of fire, an immense conflagration somewhere close by...the next, I knew that the fire was within myself. Directly afterward there came upon me a sense of exultation, of immense joyousness accompanied or immediately followed by an intellectual illumination impossible to describe. Among other things, I did not come to believe, but I saw that the universe is not composed of dead matter, but is, on the contrary, a living Presence; I became conscious in myself o eternal life. It is not a conviction that I would have eternal life, but a consciousness that I possessed eternal life then; I saw that all men are immortal; that the cosmic order is such that...all things work together for the good of each and all; that the foundation principle of the world...is what we call love, and that the happiness of each and all is in the long run absolutely certain.[1]

Whether as dramatic as the above subject's experience or much subtler, the actual awakening of the Self's awareness of its true (i.e. non-personal) identity is not the arrival of anything new as the Self is ever present.

Once realized, awareness typically then appears to expand, however gradually, so that awareness of the Self, now freed of personhood, comes to assume a more and more central position in consciousness.

Consciousness is now ready to rest more securely in itself.

---

[1] Wilber, Ken (1981). *No Boundary: Eastern and Western Approaches to Personal Growth*; p. 1.

Phase Two

Exploring The Self

Realization of the existence of and, indeed, the primacy of the spiritual dimension – which realization represents the point in our discussion at which we left off at the end of Phase One above – is only the beginning of the process of open-ended and lifelong transformation of consciousness. Following awakening to the supreme, one is subsequently free to become acquainted with that dimension. For just as coming into unexpected possession, for example, of a house or another form of property of which one had not been aware does not bring with it a familiarity with that property, further knowledge of the Self following the realization of its presence comes only by way of exploration of its nature. It is thus to the Self's gradually growing knowledge of itself that we must now turn our attention.

Chapter 8

THE SELF DISCOVERING ITSELF

Once exploration of the new territory is underway, what do we discover about this apparently mysterious dimension of ourselves which had for so long been veiled from awareness (veiled from itself, in other words)? What does the search yield? What is revealed about the nature of the spiritual?

Ultimately, of course, these questions can only be answered by each of us through our own capacities, temperamental inclinations and communication patterns. No one need set herself up as arbiter of what is valid spiritual knowledge and what is not. Nor need I regard someone else as my spiritual superior or conform to any community's collective authority.

On the other hand, spiritual knowledge does appear to be characterized by certain common features that have been reported over time regardless of culture.

For one thing, the process of becoming familiar with the spiritual dimension tends early on to begin realigning one's priorities. What the mind has always regarded as compellingly important seems to lose urgency as "seeking first the Kingdom of Heaven" (Matthew 6:33) gains ascendancy. This emerging new set of priorities sometimes leads to great shifts in certain aspects of one's life situation, including, in some cases, one's vocation and how one chooses to use one's time. Other external life situations undergo less thoroughgoing change. In all cases, though, one's interest in matters spiritual increases very significantly and eventually, sooner or later, comes to occupy central and primary importance.

So too, longstanding emotional, cognitive, interpersonal and behavioral patterns begin a gradual (in most cases), but inexorable, pattern of transformation toward non-reactivity, acceptance and an allowing of what is to simply be as one more convincingly comes to realize the necessity behind the existence of all phenomena. Eckhart Tolle has noted that consciousness, as it transforms, manifests three main characteristics: acceptance, enjoyment and enthusiasm.[1]

Understanding the necessity of all existent phenomena, of course, can just as legitimately issue in purposeful action aimed at changing circumstances in the world as it can acceptance. Indeed, detachment (or non-reactivity or acceptance) refers simply to the realization that outcomes cannot be controlled, whether one has initiated them or whether they are appearing involuntarily.

What about Free Will?

Many of us, at this point, protest that egolessness implies that I do not possess free will and subsequently jump straight to the conclusion that I must therefore be determined in my thoughts, feelings and behavior (the doctrine of determinism being, of course, the opposite of that of free will, conventionally understood) or a puppet on strings of fate.

But this objection, understandable as it is, misses the point in that it is based, once again, on the assumption that the human body constitutes, or "contains," a self that is separate from all other entities and which exercises freedom (or possesses free will, in other words). But, as has hopefully been implied in our discussion thus far, no such entity can be said to exist.

Nonduality, in other words, transcends and thus resolves the age-old debate as to whether the human is free or determined. The separate self would need to exist, after all, before it could be said to possess free will. Nevertheless, neither does nonduality imply determinism, either, as there is no self which could be determined.

Once again, it is most appropriate to resolve the issue of free will vs. determinism (or fate) by consulting our experience. It is an incontrovertible fact that we each feel a sense of freedom. And our disagreement with deterministic theories is generally based upon this sense as well as upon our innate love of freedom.

But what is it that is free? Not the body/mind (or the person) as the self which we have assumed inhabits the body and is associated with the mind is only a highly convincing fiction. Freedom is thus not a property of either the body or a supposed indwelling self or soul.

Instead, the freedom which we sense, love and wish to protect belongs to consciousness only. That we would claim freedom for a separate self only indicates that, as we have seen, consciousness has mis-identified itself with the human body/mind. Mixed with the body/mind, we not only assume ourselves to *be* the body/mind, but unconsciously claim qualities for this apparent self, such as freedom, that belong to consciousness alone.

Alan Watts has written:

> ...our intuition of free will is derived... from the fact that the Self is one with the infinite freedom, that our will is... identical with the infinite will.[2]

In short, consciousness is free and unlimited. This claim is consistent with our experience. But that freedom belongs to the One Self that we are – and which is everyone and everything – and not to a separate person, as such.

---

[1] Tolle, Eckhart (2005). *A New Earth: Awakening to Your Life's Purpose*; pp. 296-305.

[2] Watts, Alan (1972). *The Supreme Identity: An Essay on Oriental Metaphysic and the Christian Religion*; p. 113.

Chapter 9

How to Explore The Self

Let us, at this point, again briefly summarize. The chapters in Phase One of this book describe the movement of the Self from usual human consciousness, based as it is upon apparent separation from itself (separate, egoic selfhood), to awareness of itself. In the present section of this book, Phase Two, we are considering a growing familiarity with the newly discovered territory or dimension of consciousness. What I have called Phase Three – full and conscious union of the Self with itself – will be discussed in subsequent chapters. I am hoping that the present chapter, following a further brief review of our discussion thus far, will extend and build upon the Phase Two emphasis and thus promote the process of feeling, perceiving, imagining, thinking, behaving and interrelating in new ways.

Recall here that the actual conscious awareness of the Self's presence – Phase One – is itself still relatively rare among humans, though becoming less so. In most people, in other words, the universal human condition persists, which, as we have discussed, is fundamentally characterized by the Self's unawareness of even its own presence, much less any real familiarity with itself.

Returning is Allowing. Allowing is Returning

How long it took me to realize that mind and its machinations cannot bring happiness. I believed that I had come to trust God and that my will and my life were in God's hands. So where were the payoffs? I wasn't happy. This must be, I reasoned, because I hadn't yet figured out how to access the grace that the divine dimension of my being – God – was offering. And that assumption – that I must figure this conundrum out – drove years of searching *even after* initial awakening had arrived.

It was within this context that I recall watching a video of Amoda Maa giving a teaching in which she stated that it was to the Now, repeatedly during one's waking hours, that one is free to return. Returning to awareness again and again? You mean it is that simple?! No need for the mind to think about or figure this out or make it happen? Just "return and return and return," as Amoda put it? Just a shift of attention away from the objects of awareness to awareness itself?

I am quite sure that this liberating message had been presented to me many times before this. I had, for example, heard people discuss the experience of presence and had read about deliberately living in the moment. But I hadn't apparently been ready yet. I was still investing too much in the mind.

But now, finally, I had apparently suffered enough. Amoda Maa's invitation to turn toward consciousness (consciousness turning toward itself) throughout my waking hours finally came through the fog of mind. Once again, how complex is this? What do I have to understand? What preparations need to be made? What do I, as a supposed separate self, need to do? It is simply a shift, in the Now, of attention from the objective to the fully subjective.

Some people object at this point. "How am I to function in my home, my work, in my various roles and relationships and carry out my many responsibilities if I am continually trying to return attention to awareness?" Mind can be expected to argue in any way it can to keep itself at the center of consciousness.

I have found that consciousness begins to return again and again under any and all circumstances to itself. Awareness of awareness tends to remain in the background when attention is active in the realm of form. When attention becomes inactive, awareness of awareness moves into the foreground.

And there is no method to this as it is not Tom, a supposed separate entity, who is returning "his" conscious to itself; consciousness is returning to an awareness of itself on its own accord, leaving the mind-made entity, "Tom," decommissioned.

To those who say "This just sounds like mindfulness," I say: Yes, you are right. Different words and concepts perhaps, but we are pointing to the same experience.

The Caution against Ego's Return

It is important here, before we run headlong back into the illusion that I as a separate self must now undertake this exploration, to recall that the exploration of the Self is accomplished by nothing other than the Self. Once again, ego, the person, is given no part to play, as noted above. What we commonly refer to as "my will" or "my personal choice or decision" (in other words, the conventional perspective, based as it is on egoic consciousness) is neither in the lead nor being commissioned for a role; instead, becoming familiar with the Self happens by itself. We are privileged, as the Self, to witness this and to simply enjoy the process.

As Alan Watts has written:

> To ask, "How can I attain metaphysical knowledge, how can I know the infinite Reality?" is...to ask the wrong question. For if the "I" in the question is ego, the answer is that you cannot attain realization.... Perhaps, then, the form of the... question should be changed. Instead of asking how I, as ego, can attain realization, it may be that one should ask how I as the Self can attain it...This question, however, is irrelevant because the Self no more needs to realize itself than a light needs to illumine itself.[1]

We stand, thus, in the realm of utter paradox. To claim that we, as the Self (which alone is real) are *already fully arrived* at spiritual enlightenment and yet, *at the same time*, are in a process of realizing this to be true baffles and confounds the mind, which can neither reach this level nor contain it by way of words or ideas. If anything, the truth here implies a freedom from the mind and a re-birth into a new realm – that of direct knowledge of the Self.

---

[1] Watts, Alan (1972). *The Supreme Identity: An Essay on Oriental Metaphysic and the Christian Religion*; p. 166-167.

Chapter 10

MORE ON THE NATURE OF THE SELF

Our discussion thus far has centrally involved the phenomenon of awareness, which is the one universal Self. But before proceeding, let us ask ourselves the questions: "What is this awareness which I am told I am seeking? And how can it be sought other than by way of that very same phenomenon of awareness?" I am confident that answering these questions rightly will position us for deeper understanding and a more poignant experience of what it is we really want.

First, I will remind the reader that I use the terms awareness, consciousness, God, the Self and spirit interchangeably. My own preference among these terms is awareness or the experience of awareness. My explanation for preferring these terms is that their connotation, it seems to me, is more experiential than the other terms and implies a certain familiarity. We are, in other words, less likely to objectify or reify the term "awareness" and the phrase "experience of awareness" than we are "God" or "spirit," which terms, though I do use them, are for many people a bit more closed or laden with images and meanings that inevitably are based upon objectivity and otherness.

After all, who among us is not aware? To be reading these words implies that you are at this eternal Now moment experiencing awareness. If you were not experiencing awareness, you would be unable to read, hear anything or have any type of sense perception or sensation and you would have no knowledge of your thoughts or feelings. Awareness is, in short, what is always happening in you whether you consciously realize it or not. Awareness is also present in dreaming sleep or you would be unable to recount or recall dreams. But awareness is present, too, even in deep, dreamless sleep, though, because of the absence of form of any type during deep sleep (including dreams), we have no memory of deep sleep upon awakening.

Awareness is thus the irreducible aspect, or the ever-present and underlying ground of, existence, including the existence of the body/mind itself, which we typically and mistakenly take ourselves to be. Indeed, awareness pre-dates the body/mind known conventionally, in my case, as Tom and it will undoubtedly continue after this body/mind is gone.

In fact, if the entire universe of form – including space and time – were to disappear (return to its pre-Big Bang condition of non-existence), awareness, being eternal and outside of space, time and all form, would remain. Awareness thus preceded the creation event itself, which scientists tell us occurred some 14.7 billion years ago and which resulted in the appearance of form and the knowable universe. No event, after all, however primal, can happen without that event being observed, as the Copenhagen Interpretation of Quantum Physics holds. All phenomena, in other words, happens within the limitless and eternal field of awareness. No awareness. No event. *And the pure awareness which you are experiencing at this moment IS that ultimate, universal and limitless observer, which not only witnessed the Big Bang event, but of literally every event since, and which is witnessing the reading of these words at this moment.*

Therefore, for myself at any rate, the term "awareness" suggests something quite simple, experiential, continually present and, in fact, inescapable. Awareness is clearly neither esoteric nor distant and, as claimed above, is not other than the awareness that is *right now* happening in the time and place known as Tom. Awareness is even aware of the experience of being aware.

The Self as Self-Limiting

"But how is it," some people ask, "if I, as the ever-aware Self, am unlimited, I am still unable to be aware of anything in the universe beyond the relatively small social and natural environment which surrounds the body/mind along with the bodily and interior experiences of thoughts, images, sensations and emotions? I certainly do not know what my neighbor is thinking right now. Nor do I know what is going on right now in her home or at her work. How, then, am I unlimited?"

Here we must understand the nature of how pure and universal consciousness, the Self, manifests in the realm of form. Consciousness has, in first willing the existence of form and then employing the human form in order to experience duality, objectivity and otherness, voluntarily limited itself to the capacities of the human in its waking state.

As the body/mind moves into dreaming sleep, the Self withdraws from the realm of the body and the world, remaining with the mind and thus capable of witnessing the projections of mind in the dreaming state. The transition from dreaming sleep to deep sleep represents the withdrawal of consciousness from the mind, as well, and back into its specifically unlimited and infinite state.

However, as the body/mind moves back toward the waking state, first by way of dreaming sleep once again, consciousness narrows its focus within the mind, thus producing and being aware of dreams. It then narrows its focus even more as it moves toward the limitations of the body and world in the fully waking state. But the limitations of dreaming sleep and the waking state apply to the mind and body, not to the Self, to the apparent person, not to the infinite awareness that you are. Consciousness, throughout the shifts from the waking state to dream sleep to deep sleep and back again, is not itself for one moment changed or limited. There is thus a voluntary and temporary acceptance of apparent limitations on the part of consciousness, though consciousness remains, *at the very same time*, the unlimited and universal witness to all the changes that appear to be happening everywhere.

So too, looking at the question from a somewhat different perspective, following the Self's realization of its ultimate identity in the waking state (a phenomenon which, as we have noted, is currently happening in a significant percentage of humans), it doesn't immediately abandon the human form through and by which it has arrived at this knowledge. Instead, it continues to willingly submit itself to the body/mind's limitations, but now knowingly.

Here is the point at which true non-dual understanding parts ways with certain extreme tendencies, found in the outlier traditions of all religions, which reject the realm of the body and all form, viewing it merely as a distraction fit only to be escaped in favor of uninterrupted objectless awareness. Contrastingly, the non-dual tradition holds that the Self, having projected itself into form, wills, in fact, to express its infinity in the realm of the finite, thus not only enjoying the finite, but also providing the liberating knowledge of itself to as many aspects of itself (other humans in the world) as are ready to receive it and thus further expanding itself in form.

The relationship of the infinite Self to those aspects of itself still unaware of their ultimate identity is thus actually one of love and not hatred, acceptance and not rejection, and characterized by an interest in bringing all its many disparate and apparently separated aspects to itself.

This latter point is critical as it underscores, once again, the distinction between awareness, on the one hand, and that of which awareness is aware, on the other. Awareness itself is pure, transparent, without content or attributes, outside of space and time and cannot be touched, harmed or sullied in any way by anything of which it is aware. So also, awareness is that which makes knowing of all form possible – thoughts, emotions, sensations, images in the mind, people and all objects in the social and natural environments.

What's more, there are no "levels" of awareness. There is but one awareness, always and constantly shining. Awareness is present in all creatures, human and non-human, and is present, also, in the things of nature and even in so-called inanimate objects.

But despite the wide and infinite variety of phenomena and entities through and by which awareness is aware and within which it is hidden, awareness – and awareness only – is aware.

Tom, therefore, is not aware, as awareness is not a property of the brain functioning in the body/mind known conventionally as Tom; instead, awareness is aware of the brain as it, awareness, is not located in the body, as we typically assume it to be. Neither is the reader of these words, understood as an individual in her own right, aware. *Only universal and limitless awareness is aware.* Therefore, if you are experiencing awareness at this moment – and, of course, you are – then you must actually *be* timeless and unlimited awareness. Awareness is thus your ultimate identity.

The One Reality

Returning now to our question: To what am I referring by way of these various, synonymous words (among which, as noted, I prefer the word "awareness")? Obviously to nothing less than the one reality upon which form of all types is based, or is grounded in, and out of which all form emanates.

But if only awareness is aware, of what or of whom is awareness aware? In other words, what are these human body/minds? What are the things of nature? The physical objects all around us? And the non-physical objects, too, such as thoughts, images, sense perceptions, sensations and emotions?

In order to adequately answer this question, first ask yourself another, related question: Could awareness, as the one and only reality (reality being that which cannot be reduced to a more fundamental level of existence), possibly be aware of anything other than itself? The obvious answer to this question is, of course, no.

Therefore, to expand a bit upon the statement above – only awareness is aware – we might move one step further and acknowledge that awareness is always aware of nothing other than its very own self. Put another way, awareness and the objects of awareness – no matter what their surface appearances – are, as it were, ultimately the One Self. The objects of awareness are made of awareness, occur within awareness and are witnessed by awareness. Pure awareness and the objects of awareness are thus two terms that refer to the same, seamless phenomenon or process. To put it yet another way, awareness and that of which awareness is aware are opposites at the relative level that are transcended by and included within pure awareness, which has no opposite, and which cannot be known objectively. Even the experience of being aware is thus witnessed by itself! And "tat tvam asi" ("You are that").

I hope, at this point, that the questions with which we began this chapter (What is the Self, or awareness? And what is its nature?) have been satisfactorily addressed. It remains for us, however, to examine further the phenomenon of awareness in humans, as, though awareness is one and unbroken, it certainly has done and is doing a unique and novel thing by and through the human species. In humans, after all, awareness has become capable, as noted earlier, of knowing that it is aware.

Chapter 11

AWARENESS OF AWARENESS

In chapter 5, I provided a brief overview of the journey of awareness, or the Self, from its origin prior to the Big Bang creation of space, time and form of all types, into the realm of pre-egoic form and eventually into the unique and apparently dualistic experience of human existence (represented, once again, primarily by a sense of a separate body/mind self that seems to stand separate and distinct from everything and everyone that is apparently not itself, including the flow of life events). It is acknowledged, once again, that awareness has evolved, however gradually as we usually understand time, toward the capacity to "know that it knows," a phenomenon commonly termed "self-awareness" (or ego consciousness). I, Tom, can reflect upon myself – to regard or evaluate myself – with an apparent objectivity, a capacity shared by no other earthly creature.

But, contrary to the conventionally accepted philosophical and scientific view, I have also claimed that the evolution of awareness is not complete; human self-consciousness, in other words, is not the final point of the Self's journey. Awareness ultimately seeks to experience itself, by and through the human species, in the full and subjective knowledge and realization of its identity as the Self. It wills, as noted earlier, what has been called "trans-egoic" or "transpersonal" consciousness. For only transcendence re-joins, as it were, consciousness with itself following its long journey apparently away from and apart from itself. It is the point, as we have discussed, in which I overcome the apparent divide within the Self and realize that I am one, not two. What is aware of me, in other words, is the same awareness as the me that is observed.

What is the nature of transpersonal consciousness? Why is it happening – as I have claimed – to the reader of this book? We have already discussed the incapacity of the individual ego to secure the experience of ego transcendence. But can anything be done to promote it once it arrives? Or to keep it?

This chapter will address these and other questions with which the reader may be concerned. But first, now that we have identified the eternally underlying dimension of ourselves, which I mainly have called awareness or the Self, we must return to an issue which was, at an earlier point in our discussion, deferred, though its resolution has been hinted at several times already.

Who am I?

We will again confront straightforwardly the question of ultimate identity, to which we all refer by use of the pronoun "I." The reader will likely discern how discussing the issue of identity here prepares us to more productively discuss further the issue of transpersonal consciousness.

Am I a separate ego self by the name of Tom who has been visited by a dimension which, however close and intimate we have found it to be, is nonetheless still entirely other than myself? This, of course, is the mystical understanding of

God, particularly in the west. Or does the awareness that has undoubtedly always been present in, by and through this body/mind from its birth ultimately share an unbroken wholeness and essential continuity with the dimension which has now "risen up within" me?

First, consider your own experience of awareness. Does it seem, as we have all along assumed, to be contained by the body? Or, instead, does the body exist within the field of awareness? Is consciousness not conscious of the body and the sensations associated with the body? If so, then consciousness must precede, or be beyond the limits of the body (and anything else, for that matter, of which consciousness is conscious).

What about the mind, which is the other dimension or phenomenon with which consciousness identifies and so takes itself to be? Is consciousness not conscious (or aware) of the thoughts, images and sense perceptions associated with the mind? If so, then, once again, consciousness must not share the limits of the mind any more than it shares the limits of the body. As the Brihadaranyaka Upanishad puts it:

> You could not see the seer of sight. You could not hear the hearer of hearing, nor perceive the perceiver of perception, nor know the knower of knowledge.[1]

Consciousness, then, which we typically identify and closely associate with the mind and body, actually *contains* mind and body. And, if mind and body, then everything and everyone else which can be viewed as objects of some type and witnessed – namely, the world, in general.

Consciousness is thus the limitless field within which body, mind and world "lives, moves and has its very being" (Acts of the Apostles 17:28). Consciousness both preceded all form and all form emanates from out of it. Consciousness is thus the ground of all form – its basis, origin, essence and what is real about it – while, at the same time, it remains standing forever outside of both time and space, which themselves, of course, are forms.

And yet, consciousness is – at the very same time, as we have also seen – neither esoteric nor a remotely distant phenomenon; the plain and verifiable fact is that unlimited consciousness is present right here and right now in the reader of these words. If it were not, reading would not and could not be taking place in you.

Everything and everyone, in their apparent reality, thus veils or hides consciousness at their "centers," so to speak. To emphasize another aspect of the truth, we could also claim that everything and everyone is an expression of consciousness. To claim *either* that form hides consciousness or that it is an expression of consciousness is thus to speak the truth from differing angles. Obviously, there are several ways by which language can be employed to point to the nature of consciousness and form's essential identity as consciousness.

At this point, let us return to the questions identified earlier in this chapter, namely, what is the nature of transpersonal consciousness?

---

[1] *Brihadaranyaka Upanishad*, iii. 4.2. Trs. G. Thibaut; cited in Watts, Alan (1972). *The Supreme Identity: An Essay on Oriental Metaphysic and the Christian Religion*; p. 169

Chapter 12

WHAT IS TRANS-EGOIC CONSCIOUSNESS?

*T*he dualistic limitations of language, as always, prevent a linguistic capture of the experience of consciousness "coming together," as it were, with itself. Nevertheless, language can at least point to the phenomenon, references to which have already been provided in earlier chapters.

As noted above, the patient exploration of new consciousness (Phase Two) eventually leads to the insight that what I am exploring is none other than the most real aspect of myself. That the dimension of new consciousness has often, in the history of religion, been assumed to be other than me is an artifact of (largely western) cultural conditioning which projects the deepest aspect of the Self outward, thus creating a wholly separate and illusory "supreme being" who is separate from his creation.

Eastern perspectives, more aligned as they are with the actual nature of reality as confirmed in the 20th century by quantum physics, have been inclined to interpret the dimension of new consciousness as inseparable from the awareness of it, which ultimately, of course, amounts to awareness *knowing* that it is aware of nothing other than itself. Consciousness, the true I, has overcome the apparent division within itself and has identified with and as the Self. Moreover, I come to realize that awareness has all along been witnessing only itself, but, enthralled with and hypnotized by the convincing illusion of otherness, ego identity and objectivity, it simply hasn't known this to be true.

The words of Ramana Maharshi, at this point, ring true:

> There is no reaching the Self. If the Self were to be reached, it would mean that the Self is not here and now but is yet to be obtained... You are the Self; you are already That.[1]

Religion vs. Metaphysic

The Self's fully subjective and knowing awareness of itself, (which we will discuss further in Phase Three), briefly described above, is best placed into the category of metaphysic, which is an inquiry into the nature of reality.

Metaphysic, moreover, should be distinguished from religion, which is most accurately understood as being analogic to reality. Its symbols, images, sacred writings, ritual and doctrines should thus not, as theologians such as Sallie McFague and others point out, be understood literally. Instead, in its resonance with and correspondence to the content of the human psyche – phenomena termed "archetypes" by Carl Jung – religion is an externalization of inner forces. Understanding of this psychic material, its relationship to the awareness within which it appears, the meaning of the universal drama of life and liberation from those forces which promote bondage and ignorance represent the optimal functions of religion.

Since metaphysic and metaphysical realization – the latter, of course, being the central thrust of this book – and religion therefore operate on different levels, there is no essential conflict between them. Indeed, the two realms can be understood as being mutually reinforcing, liberation of spirit being the ultimate purpose of each.

But religion cut off from underlying metaphysical realization can become, as theologian Paul Tillich put it, demonic in that literal interpretations of its messages inevitably become experience distant, abstract and ideological – at distinct odds with the aims of metaphysical realization.

Thus it is that metaphysical realization can stand on its own without the augmentation of religion. But religion, arrived at in the usual way – that is, by its being passed from one generation to the next – is always in danger of becoming irrelevant or dangerous apart from the original metaphysical realization from which it once sprang forth.

Yet, it is entirely possible to approach metaphysical realization by way of religion, however few are the humans with the apparent capacity or inclination to do so.

So too, those in whom metaphysical realization is occurring may still find in religion a rich tapestry of experientially-based stories which serve to adorn and beautify the central reality of realization. Alan Watts writes:

> ...there is no conceivable conflict between metaphysic and Christian dogma, because dogma...is a perfect analogy of realization. There is no conflict between dogma and the metaphysical doctrine of the Self, because the former has absolutely nothing to say about the Self as such. In religious terminology man is the ego, and the ego is principally other

than God as it is other than the Self. Likewise, religion comprises no dogmatic definition whatsoever of the nature of consciousness.[2]

---

[1] Maharshi, Ramana (1988). *The Spiritual Teaching of Ramana Maharshi*; p. 61.

[2] Watts, Alan (1972). *The Supreme Identity: An Essay on Oriental Metaphysic and the Christian Religion*; p. 135.

Chapter 13

Growing Familiarity with The Self

*C*hapter 10 provided a description of the Self's exploration of itself, which typically begins following its awareness of its presence. And yet, a discussion of this critical phase of the Self's awakening is incomplete without attention being paid to a question that almost all of us ask at this point: "I get it intellectually. But how do I do it? How do I make it happen? And how do I hold onto it once I have obtained it?"

The current chapter will address these inevitable and necessary questions.

The Concern for Methods, Practices, Exercises and Tools Re-Visited

We first addressed the all-too-human search for the right spiritual practice in the Introduction, at which point I suggested that spiritual practice, in its reinforcement of the illusion of ego, only puts realization further out of reach.

> By their very seeking for it they produce the contrary effect of losing it, for that is using the Buddha to seek for the Buddha and using mind to grasp mind.[1]

Yet, ego, ever interested in being re-commissioned for duty, returns at any opportunity which arises. The opportunity that ego perceives following awakening to the presence of the

Self is that of taking over and putting itself in charge of the subsequent exploration of this new dimension of consciousness – what some teachers have referred to as the egoic "hijacking" of the process of spiritual transformation.

Indeed, it is ego that often raises such questions as: "How, then, do I explore what I have become aware of?" And: "How do I go about becoming familiar with this new and up-until-now hidden dimension?" In asking such questions, ego hopes to distract attention away from the immediacy of present experience of the Self. The search, once again, threatens to foil actual growth in esoteric knowledge as it focuses attention not on the eternal, limitless and timeless Now (or what Eckhart Tolle has called the "vertical" dimension of consciousness) but on finding the Self as if it were something other than one's present awareness – that is, in the realm of form (or what Eckhart refers to as the "horizontal" dimension of consciousness).

But Isn't Exploration a Form of Action?

And yet, to explore, to become familiar with, to intimately come to know strongly suggests action. Once again it seems we are faced with the dilemma of how to act without acting!

Of course, acting without acting is a logical impossibility. And ego uses this linguistic fact to its advantage as it allies itself with mind in presenting the most compelling arguments. Here, as we have seen, is the point at which it is unmistakably clear that words and language, in their correlation with mind, simply cannot capture non-dual reality – cannot, in other words, go beyond mind.

The answer, as always at the level of non-duality, is a "non-answer." Exploration of and becoming familiar with the previously hidden Self simply happens "tathata," in the original Sanskrit – or "of or by itself." Taoism, particularly as expressed by the writer (traditionally identified as Lao Tzu) of the *Tao te Ching*, uses the expression "wu wei" – meaning "non-doing" or "non-striving" – in pointing to a conscious "going with the flow" of the Tao (translated as "the way or course of nature"), which is always and forever moving in the direction it so wills.

One is, of course, always in the Tao, whether one is conscious of it or not. Indeed, "the Tao is that from which it is impossible to deviate," as it is sometimes put; one need not, therefore, accord with it. Moreover, realization of one's continuous alignment with the Tao (or "will of the One") must happen of its own accord, or by the grace of God, which means the same thing.

Obviously, ego cannot (and need not) bring about what can only happen by itself. Yet, the process of expansion can be noticed, witnessed and observed as it occurs, a phenomenon of awareness which both tends, like a spiritual catalyst, to speed up the process and to increase one's faith in it. Only experience, after all – not words, ideas and reason – ultimately convinces.

---

[1] *The Huang Po Doctrine of Universal Mind* (1947); Trs. By Chu Ch'an; p. 16; cited in Watts, Alan (1972). *The Supreme Identity: An Essay on Oriental Metaphysic and the Christian Religion*; p.70.

Chapter 14

"Tat Tvam Asi" – You Are That

In our discussion thus far, we have, among other things, examined two phases of a three-phase process of transformation.

Recall that Phase One, which principally involves a sudden awareness of a dimension of consciousness that one had heretofore entirely overlooked. On examination, this dimension turns out to be nothing less than the very awareness with and by which one has always and without interruption been aware. In short, awareness has become aware of itself in the full subjectivity and timelessness of the Now.

Also recall that, in one sense, there is nothing new in this. As noted, the human species has long been distinguishable from other species in its capacity to be aware of itself, which capacity has created the self/not-self dualism, called by Ken Wilber, as we have seen, the "primary dualism."

And yet, this awareness of awareness has now broken out of the deeply conditioned patterns of mental misinterpretation associated with the mind, which has taken the age-old human capacity to be aware that I am aware as indicating a separateness that correlates with the body-mind, a misinterpretation that creates the illusory phenomenon of ego.

In other words, upon further exploration of what seems so very new (an exploration which I have termed Phase Two, or a coming to be acquainted with this dimension that has appeared to have so spontaneously "risen up"), one comes to realize that what has appeared is not separated from conscious awareness, but is instead a "deepening" or an "expansion" of it. I realize, in short, that I am much more than I'd assumed I am and begin to question conventional understandings of my own identity.

Purgation and Illumination

It is interesting to note that the two phases briefly recapitulated above, and which we have thus far discussed, roughly parallel Phases One and Two of the three-phase process of sanctification described by several medieval mystics.

What I have called the unbidden and uncaused rising up of the Self, the mystics called "purgation," which noun has as its root the verb "purge," or to cleanse.

New consciousness does indeed seek a "cleansing" in that, as Carl Jung put it, ego is "de-centered" within consciousness, providing space for what he called a "new center" to develop. Unlike the initial and sudden rising of consciousness, the liberation of old consciousness from its apparent basis in the deeply conditioned and convincing assumption of separateness (which is ego) is generally in the nature of a process. A long period of what Eckhart Tolle has called "transition," during which consciousness alternates between egoic and trans-egoic consciousness ensues as consciousness seeks a more and more secure establishment of itself.

So too, what I have called the exploration of consciousness (Phase Two, the examination of which we are now concluding), many mystics have called "illumination," or the shining of light where there had previously been only the darkness of ignorance of one's true identity. Both exploration and illumination suggest a growing understanding (often called esoteric wisdom) of transformed consciousness or, as the mystics put it, of God, the eternal, the infinite, the supreme.

There is no guarantee, of course, that consciousness will move beyond an ongoing and chronic reaction against the arrival of the new (thus, for the current incarnation anyway, remaining at Phase One, and generating more suffering thereby) in any human. So too, should consciousness move into Phase Two, there is no certainty that, in the present incarnation, it will move beyond Phase Two.

Chapter 15

CONSCIOUSLY BEING THE WITNESS

The first answer to the question, "Who am I?," once the inner separation between phenomena of all types and what is aware of all phenomena – a separation that is implied by the Self's awakening in Phase One – is: I am the witness (or, in this context, the formless) of all form (all behavior, thought, feeling, perception, sensation and all manner of happening). I am awareness itself. As the Shankaracharya states:

> That which permeates all, which nothing transcends and which, like the universal space around us, fills everything completely from within and without, that Supreme non-dual Brahman – you are that.[1]

And since awareness, as we have seen, obviously does not originate or reside in the body as both body and mind are witnessed by awareness, I am "beyond" the body/mind or, alternatively, we could say, as noted earlier, that who I am does not share the limitations of the body/mind. I am outside of time and space. Pure. Untouched by the realm of form. I provide, in fact, the "space" within which all form exists.

Moreover, the witnessing Self is undivided, without boundary, non-local, eternal, infinite and the ultimate source and ground of form of all type. As stated earlier, it was present prior to the "Big Bang" event of 14.7 billion years ago and chose, at that precise moment in which space, time and form were created, to express itself in form. Without exception, everything is consciousness. Wayne Liquorman puts it this way: "...everything we do is in fact the happening of Consciousness – EVERYTHING."[2]

So too, the witnessing Self is changeless, constant, continuously present and, though it has been understood conventionally as a property of the brain and thus "contained" by the body, the witness underlies all form, including the body/mind, and provides form with its existence and sustenance. Though we tend to conventionally conceive of ourselves as dwelling "inside" the body, the reverse is true. Body and mind dwell in the One Self – that is, in pure, eternal and limitless awareness.

What's more, as non-dual teachers have made crystal clear, nothing and no one "has" or "possesses" awareness or is aware. The body/mind known as Tom is not, in other words, aware or conscious. Only awareness is aware. And so, since I am aware, I must *be* the One Self, the witness, pure awareness and consciousness. Within me exists not only this one body/mind, with which the Self has mis-identified itself, but all form that exists. Rupert Spira writes:

> The present now is the only now there is. The now in which the body was born is the very same now in which these words are appearing...For this reason our own being is said to be eternal...[3]

The above-described realization of one's true identity – though not complete, as we will see – is still enough to free consciousness to consciously be the witness, observer and watcher of all phenomena, both what happens "outside" the body (events in the world, other humans, the things and creatures of nature, inanimate objects) and that which happens "within" (thoughts, images, feelings, attitudes, sensations, etc.).

Perhaps consciousness, identified as it has been with the body/mind which you, as consciousness, have taken yourself to be and which has created a sense of you apart from the whole, is now ready to dis-identify from the body/mind along with the story or narrative associated with it and to identify itself with the aware witness that it is and always has been. This is the awakening of the Self to its true identity. This realization of who you ultimately are, beyond the basic knowledge of the Self's existence and even beyond becoming familiar with it, is what I have called identification with and as the Self. At this point, the Self is understood as witness, but also as the animating center of all that is witnessed.

---

[1] Devesan, P. (2013). *The Eye of the Universe: Brahmavidya Meditation and Its Upanishadic Base*; p. 27.

[2] Liquorman, Wayne (2004). *Never Mind: A Journey into Non-Duality*; p. 16.

[3] Spira, Rupert (2011). *Presence: The Art of Peace and Happiness*; p. 29.

Phase Three

Identifying With and As Consciousness

After what is often a long transition period, which, as noted above, is typically characterized by a continuous alternation between new and old consciousness, a running down of the momentum of the old tends to favor the more secure establishment of trans-egoic (literally "above and beyond" the ego) consciousness.

In Phase Three, I come to more and more consciously realize that I am far more than this body and I dis-identify from the supposed self which "inhabits" it; I am, in truth, all body/minds (and all non-human form, as well) along with the "space" of awareness within which everyone and everything exists and happens. Once again: "Tat tvam asi" – I am it.

What many medieval mystics referred to as "union," and which I have described by way of the phrase "identifying with and as the Self," thus tilts toward the full establishment of my new identity as the Self – what Eckhart Tolle has referred to as the "full flowering of consciousness."

We must now consider Phase Three – the identification of the experience of knowing, or consciousness, with the one universal and unlimited Self – in more depth.

Chapter 16

THE EXPANSION OF THE NEW SELF

The Self, as discussed in previous chapters, needs no renewal. Neither does it need expansion or progress toward a fuller or better version of itself; it has always been, and will always be, complete, absolute and in need of no improvement.

To therefore speak, as we do in this chapter, of the "expansion" of awareness represents, once again, a concession to the limited nature of language, but also an acceptance that Self-realization can, in fact, be viewed from the relative angle. Indeed, liberation *must* be considered from the relative perspective if we are to speak of it at all.

So while it is true that "we are each Buddhas from the beginning," and thus in no actual need of spiritual progress, the Self has also willed that it not consciously realize this ultimate truth of its nature until which time that it chooses to experience itself as fully established by way of a particular human. In short, for as long as you *believe* yourself to need spiritual growth, then you do "need" spiritual growth. When this apparent need has been seen through, you will be unmistakably and experientially certain that spiritual growth, as it is conventionally understood, was never really needed; *only the realization that it was never needed was needed*. Until then, it is best to keep doing what you are doing.

The Creation of a New Center

In most of us, then, ego is not eliminated all at once (though many of us are able to identify a time at which the sudden onset of transformation began). Moreover, the reduction of ego tends to be a process and might even at times give the impression that the transformation of consciousness has reversed itself and that much gain appears to have been lost in new attempts by mind, certainly not dead, to re-assert its centrality as ego. *

This can be expected. And, paradoxically, the negative evaluation of one's spiritual progress at these points, an evaluation which would suggest that, spiritually speaking, one should be "further along" or at least not caught in a state of apparent regression, is *itself* ego. It is, indeed, a particularly clever trick for ego to criticize a spiritual state or condition which ego itself has created! Ego's aim, as always, is its own strengthening and the reinforcement of its apparent indispensability, especially perhaps in matters spiritual.

---

* Mind, as I use the term, is not an entity, as such, but instead the activity of thinking, feeling, perceiving, sensing and imagining. As such, transformation of consciousness does not eliminate mind, but dis-identifies the Self from mind, thus de-centering ego, which, as I define it, is not mind, but identification with mind (as well, of course, with the body). However, some teachers use the terms "mind" and "ego" interchangeably.

Again, ego, pernicious as it is, cannot be escaped – and need not be. For all assertions on the part of ego and its very attempts to remain alive ironically serve the overall transformative process in ways that are inconceivable to ego, as the inevitable suffering brought about by ego gradually but inexorably renders egoic consciousness more and more untenable. Suffering thus brings about the phenomenon of surrender, which, in turn, prepares the way further for pure awareness - "underneath" and at the heart of all form, including ego - to become aware of itself in the ever-present Now.

This is the point, in my judgment, at which much psychotherapy and Twelve Step program work fall short of the mark in that they, however understandably, tend very strongly to pathologize or to stigmatize suffering as a personal failure on the one hand or as a "mental or emotional disorder" or "illness" on the other. This interpretation of suffering, in turn, tends to encourage a resistance to it or, similarly, a "treatment" of it. And resistance or treatment, in the attention paid to suffering which it implies and involves, only serves, paradoxically, to strengthen ego. As is true of ego itself, we cannot be rid of suffering by trying to be rid of it. Only full and unequivocal acceptance, a full allowing of it and a "going with it," serves to cut off the focus of awareness on suffering and thus the entanglement which feeds and promotes ego.

As the transformation of consciousness thus moves forward, it becomes more and more clear to consciousness that "something apparently other" than ego is now in the ascendancy. As the experience of newness, first sensed in Phase Two or even in Phase One, becomes more poignant, a "new center" of the psyche, again as Carl Jung put it, is created. Moreover, that "something apparently other," of which religion, philosophy and psychology have conceived in terms specific to each discipline, is likely still not understood to be the ever-present consciousness which is, at the same time, conscious of it.

Nevertheless, the transcending of ego has begun, and will continue for the remainder of the current incarnation. You as a supposedly separate self cannot end this process even if you decided you wanted to end it as the you which you have always understood yourself to be and which you believe could turn away from transformation is nothing more, as we have seen, than a highly convincing illusion. And an illusion, we might readily agree, cannot do, or choose not to do, anything.

Chapter 17

THE NEW IDENTITY

The "breaking through," as we put it in our discussion of Phase One, of trans-egoic consciousness – the integration and establishment of which, from the relative standpoint of time, is usually experienced as a gradual process – itself arrives quite suddenly, as we have seen, though often subtly. Moreover, the spontaneous arrival of the apparently new is simultaneous with the very beginning of the dis-identification of awareness from the separate self, or ego. This shift in consciousness represents the emergence of a new sense of identity.

It is probably by now abundantly clear that the term "new" is no more precise than are the terms "arrival" or "breaking through," as there is no "new" consciousness if the term "new" refers to something previously unknown which now replaces "old" consciousness.

Yet the terms "new" or "newness" are quite commonly employed in spiritual teachings. The terms are, though, ambiguous, as is all language when attempting to describe the infinite.

Newness and the new thus refer, paradoxically, to the realization that there really is nothing new and that what we have so desperately been seeking has been there all along, right beneath our noses, as we say. Indeed, *the awareness for which we have been seeking has been doing the seeking.* We (the One Self) seek ultimately, in other words, for nothing other than the pure awareness which is our own authentic selves, the one limitless Self. The Self, as we have discussed, is in search of itself.

Furthermore, recall from chapter 2 that the awareness with which we are aware in this eternal Now dimension is without levels, boundaries or unknown or highly rarefied regions that need to be "reached" or "achieved." Awareness is, as it is sometimes put in spiritual circles, hiding in plain view. It only requires right seeing to realize that it is fully present and that there is no need for further searching. Realization of one's supreme identity, as Alan Watts called it, also represents the freedom to identify oneself in the timeless Now with the awareness which you clearly are and to simultaneously dis-identify not only from the non-existent ego but also from the history, life situation, name and demographics associated with ego.

Who then am I?

To realize, therefore, that the pronoun "I," perhaps the most commonly spoken word in the English language, refers not to the body/mind, but to the universal, timeless and space less awareness within which this body/mind, and all form, exists is to come to the knowledge in this lifetime of your identity.

Here, then, is the answer to the seemingly futile human condition, an answer which is readily available to all "on the other side," so to speak, of the anguish of ego reduction, which reduction is necessary, as discussed above, in the process of liberation. For ego, as long as it remains central in the psyche, serves only to resist the rising up of pure consciousness. Suffering, in other words, is the fire that burns away personal selfhood, thus making the way clear for the knowing expansion of the Self in and as the psyche.

Clearly, then, the sense of completion for which the Self has destined itself to search arrives, as already noted above, through a dimension of reality of which we are typically unaware. Ego, meanwhile, plays no part in awakening except to generate the misery and unhappiness which is the precursor to awakening and which signals the incipient stage of its evolution.

That this liberation – or enlightenment, salvation, awakening, self-transcendence or whatever interchangeable term we may wish to employ – is currently occurring in a greater portion of the human population than has ever been the case should probably not be surprising. Humanity today is facing previously unknown threats to its very survival on a planet that is being relentlessly depleted of its capacity to support life by the collective egoic appetite for more. The crisis is rising, in other words, mutually with its ultimate solution: A profound shift in consciousness on the planet, the critical mass needed for which must come by way of transformation at the individual level, or from, as I sometimes put it, "the inside-out."

Hubert Benoit writes:

> When man studies himself with honest impartiality, he observes that he is not the conscious and voluntary artisan of his feelings or of his thoughts, and that his feelings and his thoughts are only phenomena which happen to him... Since I am not the voluntary artisan of my feelings nor of my thoughts I ought to recognize that I cannot be the voluntary artisan of my actions either...[1]

From Person to Pure Awareness

Let us, once again, for the sake of understanding, consider an experiential illustration of the ideas presented above.

In the time and place known conventionally as Tom, awareness seeks an awareness *of* itself followed by a full and established identification *with* itself. This shift in identity, the initiation of which, as noted above, is sudden, eventually makes it clear to awareness that Tom has always been an illusory identity created, once again, by its own identification of itself with the body/mind.

Ultimately, of course, the identification of the Self with the human body/mind is a *mis*-identification, as, though the Self (as we will see) is *both* pure awareness *and* the objects of which awareness is aware, it is never *only* this body, but *all* bodies and other forms simultaneously. Nevertheless, the Self has fully and without compulsion chosen to lose itself in this false identity – which amounts to a voluntary alienation of itself from itself - to experience objectivity, time, form and space.

The Self's transcending of its identification with ego is always entirely the decision of the Self alone and entails the realization in the now and on the part of awareness that it does not originate in the body, does not inhabit it and is not a function of the brain. Instead, the body/mind dwells, as does all form, in the universal awareness that I am, which is prior to and fully independent from the body/mind and all form and is outside both time and space.

Eventually, the universal awareness that I am, as claimed above (and to which theme we will return), comes to realize that it not only contains all form, but is the animating principle "at the center," so to speak, of all form, human and otherwise. It is thus that awareness and the objects of awareness are ultimately the same One Self. Indeed, just as only awareness is aware, only awareness is real.

Who I Am is Ever-Present

From this perspective, awareness – far from being remote, highly esoteric or available to only a small number of spiritually elite humans – is, in fact, the awareness which is always fully and eternally present. There is, in other words, simply no other awareness than that which I am experiencing currently and in this moment.

This conscious realization of the nature of awareness on the part of the One Self that I am represents, of course, universal, timeless and space less awareness becoming knowingly aware of itself in full subjectivity Awareness thus becoming knowingly aware of awareness is the birth – in, by and through a particular human organism – of what has often been called, as noted earlier, the "new self." But the new self is simply the Self in knowing and full union with itself, a union which, though it is an experience, never actually happens because there was never any literal separation to begin with.

So too – and this truth is worth repeating – realization of the Self is decidedly *not* ego's (or a separate finite self's) realization of a higher or superior Self. Recall that, since only awareness is aware, ego, in being an illusory *object* of awareness, is not aware and so cannot become aware of anything. As the title of my first book puts it, enlightenment is not, and cannot be, an ego project. Liberation is not *for* ego, but *from* ego.

Benoit, Hubert (1990). *The Supreme Doctrine: Zen and the Psychology of Transformation*; p. 29.

Chapter 18

BEING WHO YOU ARE

Given what we have already examined, it is probably clear to the reader that identification with and as the Self only *appears* to be a necessity. What, after all, has never been separated – indeed, *can* never be separated – needs no actual, literal or ontological re-unification. Indeed, there is no need to go to a place you never left or to become something you already are.

The mind, of course, in its essential duality, will never be satisfied with the paradox of an identification which never actually happens. But just as, at the quantum level, electrons can be both particle and wave simultaneously, reality is fundamentally "both-and" – that is, non-dual.

Spirit thus resonates with the subjective knowledge of its supreme identity. Moreover, liberation at this level of the psyche eventually works its way into every area of life – emotions, cognition, behavior, social interaction, the body – as consciousness in a human place and time expands.

Life is thus made new as "the old has passed away" and "the new has come" (2 Corinthians 6:17). This "second birth," as William James termed it, brings about the shift from the "sick soul" to the "twice-born personality"[1]; gratitude and humility are the natural responses. Eventually presence establishes itself with even more stability as both mind and body conform to the knowledge of the truth of our ultimate being.

Faith

It is at this point in the Self's journey back to itself that the phenomenon of faith tends to become re-defined for many people. Many of us discover that faith, associated as it is in the popular mind with intellectual assent to religious tenets, is much richer than the holding of orthodox doctrinal beliefs. In fact, faith often has little correlation to one's beliefs. We must look, therefore, to the realm of experience to understand authentic faith.

The noted 20th century theologian, Paul Tillich, placed great emphasis on the phenomenon of faith, and sought to liberate the term from the stifling connotation of religious belief for a diversifying and more secular readership

To Tillich, faith is the divine gift of openness to the newness of life in the Now, which is synonymous with the arrival of what I have called transformed consciousness. Far from the blind and uncritical clinging to religious propositions that critics of religion often associate with the word "faith," Tillich understood faith as a universal necessity for living and claimed that the alternative to this contentless experience is not freedom, but instead the unconscious placing of one's faith in one's "ultimate concern".[2] In falling short of the absolute, ultimate concerns only clutter consciousness with illusory and distracting content, or "false gods," which cannot and do not deliver salvation but another form of spiritual bondage.

For Tillich, then, genuine spiritual experience is made possible by grace through faith, which, in turn, makes possible the "acceptance of one's prevenient acceptance" – that is, the acceptance which is already fundamentally present prior to any act of the human will, decision, choice or even inclination toward God or the spiritual life.

To Tillich, the connection we seek, therefore, is willed by God, has been established by way of God's initiative, and is indissoluble. Realizing this truth, the human demonstrates in her life the "courage to be" (the title of one of Tillich's most popular books) and experiences transcendence.

Faith, then, as an openness to both life and spirit and a willingness to accept what is and to move forward with a sense of meaning is essential to human happiness.

But faith is also more than an essential or enduring attitude toward oneself, one's prospects and one's life situation. Faith, also, lifts consciousness above the realm of ego identification and replaces this old assumption as to who I am with new knowledge as to my identity.

I thus come to realize that spirit, or pure consciousness, is not only who I am but who I always have been and always will be. What's more, spirit has no past to lament, no future to fear or desire and no separate self which needs anything.

I am thus free in the eternal Now, which is not a moment in time, but the dimension upon which all phenomena is based – the timeless. In that the terms "eternal now" and the Self refer to the same dimension, I *am* the Now.

---

1 James, W. (1958). *The Varieties of Religious Experience*; p. 140.

2 Tillich, P. (1957). *Dynamics of Faith*. New York: Harper and Row.

Chapter 19

Transpersonal Consciousness vs. Transpersonal Philosophy

From the preceding brief examination of the nature of faith, we learn that it is one thing to discuss the nature of consciousness (or awareness) and even to identify everyone and everything, including myself, as consciousness. But it is another to take the next step and move from philosophy or mere doctrine and toward an experiential, heartfelt and liberating knowledge of the truth of our being. This chapter constitutes that necessary next step. What indeed are the implications for my daily life of my identity as consciousness?

First, let us once again contrast the consciousness only, or non-dual, perspective on human identity, with the conventional view. The latter, to which we all subscribe until which time the shift that is happening in us brings about realization of our ultimate identity as the Self, is based upon the unquestioned, unexamined and deeply conditioned assumption that I am a body/mind, which possesses or contains consciousness, a person, a separate self with its own history. When pressed on this, we are likely to acknowledge that we take consciousness to be a property or a function of the brain, without which there could be no consciousness.

Even spiritually-oriented discourse betrays a basic misidentification when we speak of "my ego" or "my awareness" as there is ultimately no person which could or would possess an ego or awareness. Such formulations are, therefore, rooted in dualistic assumptions regarding my identity.

Misunderstanding on the part of consciousness as to its identity thus creates, as we have seen, the illusion of separate selfhood, ego and ego-based consciousness. It also projects a world and a separate supreme being. Moreover, to assume that I as a separate self "am conscious" also prioritizes ego (the separate self) over awareness, out of which ego is made. The true nature of awareness thus remains fundamentally distorted by the thinking and interpreting mind.

But, consistent with the perspective described already in these pages, universal and unlimited awareness is who I am and who I have always been. The pronoun "I," in other words, refers not to a body/mind or to the illusory, fictional and ego-based "person," which seems to inhabit the body, but to the timeless and space less awareness, present before all worlds, which grounds all form and which is, at the very same time, playing the parts of all form, as noted earlier, in a universal *maya* (once again, a Sanskrit word meaning play or drama). There is, in other words, nothing other than God, who alone is real. John Greven writes:

> The Tao is... what you truly are.... What you are is not a thing or object that the mind can grasp...the mind is of no use for realizing your true nature...*what you are is not a thing or object that the mind can grasp*...Has the mind made a mistake in identity? Are you perhaps something outside of the limited mind? Are you the source and, as such, cannot be known by the appearance? We believe that we are a person

with these attributes, problems and suffering because we, as the ego, believe what the mind is telling us. If you are a timeless being, then the very foundation that this person is built on...is a lie. The idea that you were born and that you will die...is a lie. But how can the ego get rid of ego? It can't...the unreal – the lie – is effortlessly dropped as the false center...There is nothing you can do to discover your true nature. Remember, what you are is not in hiding, just overlooked by the mind. The seeming power... of the ideas and concepts evaporate...when seen as false. In the removing of false ideas, the supreme subject becomes...apparent, although it is always bright and shining.[1]

Described, then, from the objective, relative third person perspective, the essence of everything and everyone is consciousness and each entity is an aspect of the whole. Yet, from the subjective, first person – the perspective to which and from which ultimate truth is revealed and expressed – each human can truthfully say "I am unlimited and eternal consciousness." And recall that there are not numerous "I's" or numerous selves to which the pronoun "I" refers. Instead, there is but one "I" which refers, of course, to the One Self. Jesus says as much in the New Testament. "I and my father are one" (John 10:30). "When you have seen me, you have seen the father" (John 14:9). "I am the way, the truth and the life...." (John 14:6). Each of us can validly say the exact same things about ourselves, as these "I" statements are as true when spoken in the time and place known as Tom, Dick or Mary as they were in the time and place known as Jesus. The Self is the same in all.

Transpersonal Consciousness as Transformed Consciousness

I have attempted to point out in this chapter the distinction between transpersonal philosophy and transpersonal experience. In so doing, we are further addressing the question: What is transpersonal consciousness?

Let us proceed along these lines and examine the issue with a turn toward the actual phenomenon of transformed consciousness. As has been my aim from the beginning of this book, we will prioritize experience over theory, abstraction and all forms of false authority.

First, transpersonal consciousness proceeds from out of the (usually) gradual expansion of awareness implied in Phases Two and Three of transformation. Eventually the growing awareness of and familiarity with the Self, which characterizes Phase Two, tilts decidedly in the direction of an actual identification with and as the Self (Phase Three). The spiritual (or noetic or esoteric) knowledge that comes by way of Phases Two and Three naturally issue in a more ongoing and established experience which is correlated with the Self's liberation.

Having, then, discussed the three phases in terms of knowledge acquisition, we must now turn to a description of the ongoing experience of liberation itself. What really is transpersonal consciousness? How do you know when it has arrived? How will you know when it has more fully established itself? What does transformed consciousness feel like, subjectively, "from the inside"?

Much has already been presented regarding life after initial awakening. Our examination of Phases Two and Three, after all, described the expansion of consciousness following its "rising up" (also known, of course, as its initial "awakening").

And yet, having become relatively stable (in Phase Three) following the long period of transition from egoic to trans-egoic consciousness (Phase Two), what further can be said about the experience of consciousness as it becomes more and more established? Adyashanti puts it this way:

> When our personal will has broken down, a whole different force comes rushing into our system. It's the force of spirit, and it can now become operational because we are no longer avoiding it through grasping at personal will...a rebirth happens...we start to be moved by the completeness and totality of life itself...you start to get a feel for how willfulness is replaced by a sense of flow. [2]

I believe it to be critical to keep in mind that, as so many spiritual teachers have claimed, it is impossible to speak knowingly of the Kingdom of Heaven from outside of it. Suffice it to say, therefore, that "experiencing is believing," and that, once again, your own fully subjective experience should be viewed as the primary authority. Spiritual teachers can only reinforce what is already happening by way of you; they can neither initiate it nor can they provide direction on how to more fully realize it as there are no methods that can bring you to a consciousness that is already fully present. Nor are such methods necessary.

For many of us this is a liberating realization as, if no one can bring about that for which you and I are searching, then neither do we *need* anyone in any ultimate sense. I am already there. I am already *it*. And this truth is prior to any thought or idea about it, including the thoughts "I need to get this" or "I need to keep this."

The mind, of course, which can be expected to oppose liberation at every turn, will object: "But how do I come to realize that I am already there or, indeed, that I am already it? And how do I hold onto it once I have achieved it? Don't I need assistance?" The mind can be expected to draw us into these infinite regressions at every turn.

Again, the true spiritual teacher might answer: "Yes, I am here to help. But my 'help' comes in the form of pointing out to you that you don't need help – which is, of course, really not help in the usual sense of the term."

Just as all liberating psychotherapy ultimately serves the purpose of revealing to the client that he does not actually need psychotherapy, all authentic spiritual teaching, practices and teachers themselves have as their purpose the freeing of the apparent person (who you take yourself to be, in other words) – a freedom which implies the falling away of all methods and masters. True spiritual teaching is paradoxical in that it is not conventional teaching in the sense of passing on content, but instead encourages the subtractive process inherent in the transformation of consciousness itself. In short, teachers and teaching, if they are genuine, seek to make themselves unnecessary.

[1] Greven, J. (2005). *Oneness: The Destination You Never Left*; pp. 25-29.

[2] Adyashanti (2008). *The End of Your World: Uncensored Straight Talk on the Nature of Enlightenment*; pp. 155-156.

Chapter 20

THE KINGDOM OF HEAVEN

Let us continue here with the subjective emphasis which prioritizes one's actual lived experience of transformed consciousness. In so doing, it is instructive to further consider the metaphor for transpersonal consciousness which Jesus uses repeatedly in the New Testament of the Bible – the Kingdom of Heaven (or of God). What does it mean to be "inside" the Kingdom of Heaven? Is it even possible to be outside of it? And does this metaphor sufficiently describe transformed consciousness?

First, the Kingdom of Heaven refers to the actual experience of consciousness itself (not to the objects of consciousness), which is facilitated by the expanding knowledge of one's identity as the Self. In short, as identification with the Self (and the corresponding dis-identification from ego) becomes more stable, one's experience feels new. This new, and eventually more abiding consciousness, has been called many things, as noted earlier: trans-egoic consciousness, transpersonal consciousness, new consciousness among others. The Kingdom of heaven is thus simply another, very ancient, linguistic pointer to this dimension of experience.

It is important, I believe, to reiterate here that the various qualities which distinguish transformed consciousness from egoic consciousness proceed naturally from out of transformed consciousness; they are not the cause of it. Nor are these qualities the cause of the expansion or deepening of consciousness as the latter more and more identifies with and as the Self. They are not themselves the key to the door of heaven and cannot be used to enter it. Indeed, recall that one does not and cannot enter the Kingdom of Heaven by way of any method, even that of imitating the qualities often associated with it.

It is, of course, human nature to, in this way, "put the cart before the horse" or to "try making the tail wag the dog," two sayings by which we attempt to capture the tendency we humans demonstrate in our ego-based and futile efforts at seizing happiness.

Indeed, to realize that one is thus attempting to take the Kingdom of Heaven "by force" (Matthew 11:12) *is itself* awakening and so provides needed evidence to the apparent human seeker that the transformation for which she seeks is *already happening* without it needing to be initiated by a supposedly separate, conscious human will.

Moreover, since, as also noted earlier, only realization of one's rootedness in the Kingdom of Heaven provides the capacity to speak knowingly of it, we are free to allow consciousness to speak through us without obstruction from ego.

There is, in other words, no longer need (there never actually was need, of course) to deliberately act, to behave with purpose or with calculation or to attempt a controlling of outcomes. As the spontaneity and freedom of the Self comes to further marginalize ego (or the "old self") the Self is observed (by none other than itself) as acting with self-abandonment and freedom. Will and action are seen to be ultimately the same phenomenon.

The mind, in other words, with its emphasis on objectivity, cannot experience the Kingdom of Heaven. Only "the heart," which capacity has been provided by awakening, can know the Kingdom of Heaven.

The Kingdom of the Mind versus the Kingdom of Heaven

It is probably clear to the reader that entrance into the Kingdom of Heaven is, simultaneously, a liberation from what could be called the Kingdom of the Mind or Ego. The Kingdom of the Mind is also the Kingdom of the World as the realm of mind, body, world and all form are mutually correlated with each other. As Jesus points out in John 18:36, "My kingdom is not of this world."

It must be reiterated again that identification with the body, mind and world is not a spiritual pathology as such. Indeed, identification with the body/mind is the usual human condition. Virtually all normally developed humans beyond about age two years enter this realm of illusion and remain, as David Hawkins puts it, "hopelessly trapped in its illusory house of mirrors." [1]

This, then, is the Self in apparent bondage – a bondage in which ego must forever appease, control, resist and appropriate a realm which is decidedly other and certainly not me. The realm of objects – whether they be people, circumstances, relationships, one's own feelings and thoughts, states of mind – continually presents both threat and opportunity, triggering in consciousness either reaction or attempts at exploitation.

As living based on fear and desire gains momentum, suffering increases, touching every area of life, corrupting the apparently separate will itself and driving it further into clinging, on the one hand, or resistance on the other, a self-perpetuating cycle that cannot be broken at the level at which it is being produced.

Such is the nature of the human condition, or, as I have called it, the Kingdom of the Mind. There is no need to criticize ourselves for the human condition or fight against it as its existence has itself been necessary as the Self awakens. But neither is it ultimately real and its falling away is inevitable.

Realization, not Achievement

Once again, we must return to a central theme in our discussion: That transformed consciousness is not an achievement resulting, as I put it in my first book, from an ego project. Liberation is instead the outcome of realizing what is and always has been the truth of who I am.

If this be so, then it is not possible to ever actually be outside the Kingdom of Heaven. As Alan Watts wrote, "one cannot deviate from the Tao."[2] The objection to this, of course, is that, if the consciousness known as the Kingdom of Heaven is the state of consciousness which arrives naturally because of my realizing that I am *already in* the Kingdom, then to not be experiencing this quality is to be outside the Kingdom.

Here is the point, as the reader has perhaps surmised, at which we risk going around in endless circles. And yet, the truth, as always, is quite simple: The quality of consciousness which is the Kingdom of Heaven *is identical to* my true eternal being, the Self (or pure consciousness). The Self that I ultimately am, in other words, is always and eternally at peace, ever experiencing the joy of its pure being, fully aware without interruption of itself and one with itself, even at those times when emotional distress, discord and dysfunction seem to be in the ascendancy. These typically unwanted experiences are happening in the realm of ego, not at the level of who I ultimately am.

This in no way implies a suppression of the experience of suffering. In fact, quite the opposite. Since I am privileged to know myself to be the eternal, the infinite, the supreme – that which remains untouched and unaffected by any and all experiences – I am free to allow experience to happen in me and to me fully and without resistance.

Realization of my ultimate identity as the Self (the vertical dimension) thus frees me from the need to resist what happens at the levels of ego, body and experience in the world (sometimes, as noted earlier, called the objective, or horizontal, dimension).

This freedom, which can be described using any number of words – acceptance, non-reactivity, non-resistance, allowing, surrender, letting be – not only enables a joyful engagement with life despite circumstances, it also denies our sharp emotional and mental reactions the feeding they receive from our resistance to them. In other words, my resistance to my feelings, attitudes, thoughts, and behaviors only strengthens them. The fight, in short, perpetuates the problem.

Allowing thoughts, feelings and behaviors to happen in all their compulsivity and obsessiveness leads, therefore, to their gradually losing momentum. Moreover, the energy which has been trapped in these autonomous patterns are thereby liberated to rejoin the whole of the Self. Thus does the Self appear to be made whole again (a wholeness which it, of course, never really lost) and the experience which, once again, proceeds naturally from the realization of primal wholeness is peace, joy, and the love which is the outgoing expression of this deep inner experience.

---

[1] Hawkins, David R. (2011). *Dissolving the Ego, Realizing the Self: Contemplations from the Teachings of David R. Hawkins MD PhD*; edited by Scott Jeffrey; New York City: Hay House; p. 63.

[2] Watts, Alan (1991). *Nature Man and Woman*; p. 121.

Chapter 21

PRESENCE

We have already discussed the nature of both the human condition and awakening from it, particularly in this book's presentation on Phase One. Yet, as the expansion of awareness never comes to an end in any human lifetime, another perspective on the process of liberation might be helpful at this point.

As it further establishes itself as the new center, a center previously occupied by ego, consciousness becomes more and more intimately known to itself. This growing consciousness of consciousness, in turn, makes it plain that the consciousness with which we are conscious has always been present and, in fact, hasn't changed even while the realm of form, including the body/mind, has been in a state of continuous change. Increasingly, then, one identifies with awareness rather than with thinking, a shift which issues in freedom from the bondage to ego.

As one experiences release from suffering at both the level of mind and body, one realizes that she is seeing past illusion and falseness and can rightly think and so rightly act. Again, one has come to live, as we discussed in the previous chapter, more knowingly in the Kingdom of Heaven, having entered a realm in which there is only ever the eternal Now.

What's more, no "grand strategy" has been needed or has guided this transformation. No additions were required. No acquiring of that which was not already present. No tools. No methods. No practices. No techniques. No ego-based action whatsoever. Only realization. And this by the grace of God, a phrase which is synonymous with the expansion having happened on its own accord. It has occurred, in other words, by itself. The expansion of presence is thus, as has been stated, a subtractive process, as ego is more and more deflated, lessened, and marginalized.

Tony Parsons has written:

> Presence is our constant nature...Only here in present awareness of simply what is can there be freedom...Presence is totally effortless and is nearer to me than breathing...In allowing presence...we embrace a kind of death. What dies is all expectation, judgment and effort to become...What dies is the dream of individuality. [1]

Presence, then, refers to the unlimited and eternal nature of awareness, which does not share the limited and finite nature of the body/mind.

---

[1] Parsons, Tony (1995). *As It Is: The Open Secret to Living an Awakened Life*; pp. 37-39.

Chapter 22

Spiritual Knowledge

Contemporary humans are strongly conditioned to associate the term "knowledge" with either rational thought (or reason) or with the outcomes of the empirical scientific method (research, data, the realm of the sensory). These are the two levels, as Ken Wilber has pointed out, that are generally recognized as producing legitimate knowledge.

And yet, prior to the modern era in the West (before about 1600), knowledge of a spiritual (or esoteric) nature was also affirmed as valid. Spiritual knowledge, which is facilitated not by the mind or the senses but by intuition, was understood as originating at a level deeper than both mind and senses – at the level of spirit, or God. The phenomenon of spiritual awakening implies a re-affirmation of spiritual knowledge (or to use Kant's term, "noetic" knowledge).

Spiritual knowledge – called in antiquity "gnosis," a term appropriated by the Gnostics to describe their main concern – cannot be taught in the usual manner that reason and empirically-based knowledge is transmitted, which is, of course, by way of language and ideas. Instead, spiritual knowledge arises from within, which is to say by way of the purely subjective, and thus is more akin to what, as noted earlier, might be called "wisdom." One simply comes to know truths about reality, oneself and God and this knowledge, moreover, rises spontaneously and by its own accord in the time and place of its choosing.

So too, it is important to distinguish spiritual knowledge from religious doctrine. The latter can be believed or disbelieved; spiritual knowledge is, as the word implies, what one knows, not what one believes. The experiential aspect of coming to know in this way brings with it, in other words, a certainty of its truthfulness that typically cannot be shaken.

And yet, for all its experiential veracity, spiritual knowledge cannot be captured in language or by way of ideas, as spiritual knowledge, by its nature, is non-dual. As the Zen master said, "You cannot capture the non-dual in a dualistic net." Thus, it is that words and language, dualistic nets as they are, can only point to what is ultimately real.

Esoteric wisdom, as we have seen, arrives in the very first wave of awakening, during which one comes to realize that pure and eternal awareness is distinct from that of which it is aware. Divine knowledge then expands, once again as we have seen, as awareness, in Phase Two, becomes gradually more and more acquainted with itself.

In Phase Three, divine knowledge is characterized by the theme of identification with awareness, the knowledge of who I am. Not only do the fresh and new perspectives on everything from my identity to the nature of the human will to life's purpose to the joy of living in perfect freedom enrich my own experience as the process of transformation continues, I am privileged to share them with others, thus allowing the body/mind to be a sort aperture through which the truth goes out into the world and the light shines in the darkness.

More and more my life is given over to the purposes of the Self, which appear to be centered on the establishment and expansion of Self-realization by and through humans.

But it is critical to remember that esoteric knowledge is not knowledge of any form or type of object – which is the nature of conventional knowledge – but instead is the knowledge of what it is that is aware by way of a totally subjective experience of itself, coming entirely from within. Though philosophical concepts designed to point to the truth can be passed on from one mind to the next, the actual *experience* of the truth cannot be prescribed, made to happen in oneself or others and occurs entirely on its own accord.

We need not, in other words, accomplish or do this in the usual sense of the terms. And, since awareness becomes aware of itself entirely by itself – or by the grace of God, which means, as we have seen, exactly same thing – we can trust the process and observe it happening. The Self is viewing itself acting, perceiving, having sensations, imagining, feeling, thinking and behaving in the world.

It will not be long before one realizes that being aware of the experience of knowing – and living in the Now based on that awareness – renews every aspect of one's experience. Consciousness resonates effortlessly and egolessly with consciousness. In my esoteric knowledge, I am freed from illusion, enabled to let go of dependencies, become disentangled from form of all types, dis-identify from the mind-made self and the story of me and enjoy openness and limitlessness. This is the omega point of consciousness.

How, then, does one come to know the spiritual dimension if one cannot know it by way of concepts or ideas?

This question frames a contentious issue, especially in the context of western religion, which has looked upon reports of personal and direct experience of the divine (or the spiritual) dimension with suspicion. And yet, there have been – and are – mystics in all times, places and cultures whose claims to direct experiences of the divine have been compelling, sometimes even sought out.

This level of knowing, then, mediated by way of intuition, is fully subjective. And subjectivity can be interpreted in different ways. While St. John of the Cross or Theresa of Avila are understood as describing subjective experience simply because they speak of an inner, numinous and indefinable God, the subjectivity of a Hindu implies, as does the thesis of the present book, that the experience of knowing is the infinite itself and that it, moreover, is the only reality.

Chapter 23

THE RETURN OF OLD CONSCIOUSNESS

The strong tendency to seek in the realm of form for an experience, relationship, achievement or state of mind which one hopes will bring all suffering once and for all to an end continues for a time, given the momentum behind it, even following awakening. The deeply conditioned patterns of consciousness which apparently "go out from themselves" to find happiness, in other words, survive the initial awakening of consciousness to itself and continue their compulsive search. These tendencies can, at times, still show up even in Phase Three, as identification of consciousness with itself can leave behind remnants of the old.

For while it is true that consciousness, at this point, has given up on finding what it wants in the more overt realms of the objective world – wealth, prestige, social status, attention, worldly power and the like – it very well might not have given up entirely on the subtler realms of that world. Insights, feelings, states of mind and intellectual formulations of reality such as elaborate cosmologies often replace the grosser levels of the objective. And yet, the principle which drives the search remains the same even while the objects to which one aspires, or to which one becomes attached, have changed markedly.

This continuation of the search following initial awakening and often long after is probably inevitable given the strength of the conditioning which propels it. What's more, in a very real sense, there is nothing one, as ego, can do to speed up the process of going beyond these now much diminished but still present tendencies. Ironically, to believe otherwise and to attempt a deliberate transcending of them is to reinforce consciousness in its continued identity as a separate self which must transcend old patterns of futile spiritual searching. Fortunately, as always, there is nothing which one, as an individual, needs to do either, as the fading away of ego-based attempts to find or achieve happiness in the objective realm happens of its own accord as consciousness becomes ever less and less enthralled by the world of objects, however sublime and thus compelling and attractive they might remain.

As limitless consciousness, one is free to be aware of oneself in any and all circumstances and in this simplicity lay an important truth: It is in the continuous willingness of consciousness to return again and again to itself that liberation from the hypnotic power of the realm of objectivity is gradually lessened and not in a once-and-for-all perfect answer.

What, then, following a sufficient, if imperfect, establishment of consciousness in Phase Three identification, can one expect? Simply this: The repeated return of awareness to itself. Again, and again. For there is nowhere else it needs to be. Under any and all circumstances, consciousness is simply free to return to the vertical dimension, that "back and down" movement of consciousness which more and more replaces the horizontal dimension of seeking happiness in the realm of objects and form. Nothing more complex than that. Nothing for ego to revel in while deluding itself that it is achieving enlightenment. No elaborate methods. No grand revelations. No perfect formulations of non-dual philosophy. No definitive or dramatic breakthroughs in time or space. Only the simple return – again and again and again – of awareness to a subjective awareness of itself.

The great 20th century Indian sage, Sri Ramana Maharshi, called this return to the Self in the immediacy of the present moment "Self-inquiry," which is simply an asking of various versions of the question "Who am I?" under any and all circumstances. One might, for example, ask of oneself: "Who is it that feels this way?" or "Who is it that would have acted any differently?" or "Who is it that is thinking and who is it that is aware of the thinking?" Ramana's Self-inquiry is designed, therefore, to expose the supposed separate feeler, doer or thinker to be illusory and to simultaneously reveal the truth that the One Will is happening always and everywhere, in what one does and in what happens to oneself. For none other than the limitless One Self is real. And everything that happens is designed to awaken the Self from the hypnosis of false identity and to identify itself with eternal awareness itself.

It is not hard to understand why so many spiritual people find the truth of their being to be simplistic or otherwise unpalatable. Ego, after all, plays no role in this phenomenon, and even spiritual people remain invested in ego long after initial awakening. So too, as we have seen, there is no method to Self-realization that can be mastered. It doesn't require arduous preparation, the right belief system or strenuous effort. Moreover, ego is offended by its de-commissioning and insulted by there being no hierarchy of truth, no privileged in-group, no conditions or qualifications for it to meet and no spiritual elite with whom to identify. Simply the return of consciousness again and again to itself.

This continuous and repeated return of consciousness to itself in the immediacy of Now represents, in its subjectivity, a reversal of the usual movement of the egoic human condition from a "going out" from itself to a "coming home" to itself - to the dimension of faith. What's more, the repeated return of consciousness to itself comes to more and more characterize the nature of consciousness, which had up-till-now been dominated by an absorption in objectivity and form. In other words, one comes to abide, as consciousness and not as a separate self, more and more in the peace of the eternal, the timeless, the infinite. And lest one be tempted to assume that this abiding in transpersonal consciousness represents a trance state, it should be remembered that awareness of awareness *increases* the capacity for concentration, attention to detail, functioning in the world and responding naturally and spontaneously to one's social and natural environment.

Of course, no one is entirely convinced of the truth of one's identity as the infinite and the implications of this truth until one becomes ready to partake of it in one's immediate experience. Experience, once again, is the primary teacher. And the experience of awareness in the timeless Now is open to anyone at any time.

Ego, of course, can be expected to ask: "Okay, sounds good. How do I do this?" Ego knows, after all, that to survive it must distract consciousness with questions of method, as we tend to assume that, to become aware of awareness and then to maintain that awareness, an "outside-in" prescription or practice must be applied by a separate me.

But the ego mind's questions, its objection and its accusations all exist in the realm of objectivity. This doesn't imply that mental activity is bad or wrong. It doesn't even imply that identification with mental activity, the human phenomenon that creates ego, needs to be directly attacked or eliminated. Yet, that ego and its identification with thinking exist in the dimension of objective form *does* make it relative. And, if relative, then incapable of entering the dimension of the eternal and ultimate. Only the eternal can know the eternal.

And so, no matter what might be happening in the realm of the mind, body and world, we are free in the Now to return to the realm of awareness time and time again.

While it is thus true that the way to true happiness is narrow – pure awareness, indeed, can be found only in the eternal Now – it is not an ego accomplishment, spiritual feat or grand achievement. The process can, in a very real way, be left to consciousness to accomplish. This, of course, could be called the element of trust and is a key feature in the transformation of consciousness.

Yet, as we have seen, neither is awakening and post-awakening expansion a passive process in the usual sense of something or someone other than me doing the actual work. I as the Self do the work, but not I as a person. Ego, as such, can do, and need do, nothing. All the while the true Self is accomplishing the transformation of consciousness outside the conscious awareness of the body/mind. But this Self is me, not an outside agency, external God or supreme being. My will is its will. I *am* the Self.

Chapter 24

GRATITUDE

The natural outcome of realizing my identity as the One and Only Self – a realization which, as it were, "lifts" me above the old separate self identity while preserving legitimate and necessary mind functions such as sensing, feeling, thinking, imagining and perceiving – is gratitude and its sister, humility.

What seeker would not experience thankfulness upon realizing that she is free? That he is eternal? And who would not, along with that thankfulness, be humbled in knowing that this realization is not an achievement – that I, as Tom, did not, and could not, have ever attained this? That it has come from another dimension – call it God, the Deep Self, pure awareness or whatever you may prefer. You don't have to call it anything if you don't want to.

As consciousness becomes gradually less prone to more than relatively brief returns to old, object-based consciousness, the body/mind system continues to adjust to transpersonal consciousness and becomes more settled, clear, non-reactive and relaxed. Many people report a new sense of lightness as the dead weight and compulsivity of the human condition lifts.

Consciousness, in fact, becomes ever more sensitive to returns to the old so that such returns tend to become less frequent and shorter in duration. Indeed, the sudden realization in the Now that a return to egoic consciousness has occurred is, in fact, the liberation from it. No methods are needed. All can be left to consciousness.

Giving of My Abundance

Virtually all authentic spiritual traditions have put great emphasis upon service to one's neighbor and/or to the natural environment. Whether associated with the rubric of love or compassion, genuinely reaching out to, and being present for, others is proclaimed to be of vital and central importance to the truly spiritual life.

Wholistic understandings of the spiritual life, such as the present book, is no exception. It is thus important that we examine, in this section of our discussion, how the foundational experience of awakening and the process of transformation empowers consciousness, now freed from the tyranny of ego, to give from out of its infinite abundance of spiritual riches.

As previously noted, ego-centric consciousness tends very strongly toward the view that other humans are either threats or opportunities. Ego-centeredness is, after all, a sort of bondage to the realm of form and so to be able to effectively control and manipulate the realm of form is essential for a sense of wellbeing, however fleeting this sense inevitably is.

Notions of service to others are thus tainted by egoic consciousness and is interpreted by ego as, at best, a command or a mandate and is thus grudgingly and without genuineness engaged in as one might obey any other requirement; or it is ignored altogether.

The shift from ego-consciousness to God-consciousness – a process described, as we have seen, by way of three discernable phases of transformation – affects all areas of life, including that of one's relationships with other people. Living in the Kingdom of Heaven is a de-centering of ego and creates a new identity, relieving consciousness of egoic interpretations of the other as threat or opportunity. Others no longer threaten as there is no vulnerable ego to be threatened. Nor are others viewed as opportunities as there is no longer any need for ego reinforcement or feeding.

No longer either fearing others or needing them, consciousness is enabled to respond in love to any and all with whom one might interact. This is freedom in outgoing action, a generous providing to others from out of one's unlimited abundance with no need for investment in the outcomes of one's service. This, then, is love – the externalization of the inner experience of transformation.

And how well service to others integrates with the Self's ultimate purpose in humans – to knowingly know itself – as once the Self comes to realize its identity by way of a human form it develops the capacity to see itself everywhere and as everything and everybody. True and conscious partnership and relationship with all life forms thus reinforces the tantric emphasis discussed in chapter 3. "I am what there is and all that there is," said Alan Watts. And I am everything and everybody. "Love your neighbor as yourself" says Jesus in the gospels. Loving one's neighbor as oneself ultimately means loving one's neighbor as oneself because one's neighbor is oneself. And the Self's love for itself is of its very nature. Love, in other words, is not merely an attribute of the Self any more than peace is an attribute of the Self. The Self *is* love and peace.

Love and compassion, then, imply giving from the riches of my heart rather than viewing others as the sources of those riches. This, as we have seen, is what Eckhart Tolle, Amoda Ma and others refer to as the vertical focus (down and into oneself) and its arrival gradually ends the horizontal focus (endless searching in the realm of form), which characterizes ego conscious prior to awakening. Serenity, after all, can only be found in the Now, which is the locus of the vertical focus, and will never be found "someday," the future orientation being correlated with the horizontal emphasis on getting and holding onto. Indeed, serenity implies freedom from the strategies of obtaining and the anguish of living for, and on behalf of, ego.

There is, in the end, no one "out there" to either despise or cling to, to be afraid of or to resent. No one has ever done anything or could do anything to me or against me. As Jeff Foster asks: "….is there really any separation between us? Is this separation not just a construction of thought? Are we not the same, you and me?" [1]

There is only me. Not, of course, in the role of Tom Galten, which is only illusory. There is only the One. And I am that.

---

[1] Foster, Jeff (2007). *Beyond Awakening: The End of the Spiritual Search*; p. 80.

Chapter 25

CHOOSE CONSCIOUSNESS OVER FORM

From the very beginning of our lives we are trained by our culture to view the world, which apparently exists "around us," as what is most real. Meanwhile, the dimension of awareness, which alone is aware of the realm of form, is unaware of its true nature and identity. Our culture, as a collective whole, is pre-Phase One – that is, it has not yet entered the phase in which consciousness in a sufficient number of people has come to realize that it is distinct from that of which it is conscious.

It is due to this apparent radical difference between those individuals in whom awareness has become aware of itself and thus has entered the three-stage process of transformation, on the one hand, and the collective consciousness of our culture, on the other, that awakening is a subversive phenomenon. Not subversive in the ordinary sense of political or social revolution. But subversive nonetheless, in that one's values and priorities tend to diverge markedly from that of the culture. One is becoming more and more acquainted, and identifying more and more, with that dimension which the mind can neither approach nor attain. Our culture, in short, is ego mind at the collective, macro level.

Some non-dual spiritual teachers have suggested that the current world order is destined to be replaced by transformed consciousness at the collective level. Eckhart Tolle and others have suggested that expanding consciousness, upon reaching critical mass at the collective level of society, will touch off a shift toward what Eckhart has called the new earth. He writes:

> Is humanity ready for a transformation of consciousness...? The possibility of such a transformation has been the central message of the great wisdom teachings of humankind. The messengers – Buddha, Jesus and others, not all of them known – were humanity's early flowers... A widespread flowering was not yet possible at that time... Is humanity more ready now than at the time of those early teachers?... Not everyone is ready yet, but many are, and with each person who awakens, the momentum in the collective consciousness grows, and it becomes easier for others.[1]

My current presentation is too limited in scope to discuss the phenomenon of collective consciousness and its potential for undergoing a shift at the macro level that parallels transformation at the individual, micro level. Suffice it to say that, though the way of liberation is, as M. Scot Peck said some 40 years ago, still very much "the road less travelled",[2] momentum is moving in that direction. Moreover, the shift of consciousness has implications for collective, as well as for individual, consciousness.

Knowingly Be the Self

Though sorrow, fear or anger might very well rise in us at times over our apparent alienation from this world, the reward which steadily comes as we become more and more "individuated," as Jung put it, and as consciousness becomes ever more capable of remaining in the peace of its true nature, precludes any regrets.

Indeed, there is no need to conform to the world by giving it one's primary attention. Primary attention can instead be given in any and all circumstances, to the Self - that is, to the simple experience of knowing. Return again and again to that pure consciousness, the dimension of being aware, and it will eventually be clear that the return is happening entirely by itself and of its own accord. While there undoubtedly will be situations that draw attention away from the Self, even to the point of becoming lost again in the realm of form, waking up from these now temporary falls into unconsciousness is promised. In fact, as noted earlier, the very realization in the moment that one has been lost in form *is itself* the waking up from it. These periods of entanglement will become less and less frequent, less and less intense and will also decline in duration as the process of transformation continues in you.

You are free to notice this expansion of awareness, as expansion is further promoted by its own awareness of itself. More and more there is joy in this awareness of awareness. This joy, in turn, encourages further trust in the process. The process is who you are. And it will not stop. It is the peace which the world in no way can come even close to giving us. And, though we need not harbor hostility toward the world, neither do we any longer need it for our happiness.

To illustrate this point, let us consider the following metaphor. A boat which is tied by a strong, thick rope to the shore will not, under even the stormiest circumstances, be swept out to sea. The boat may at times drift closer to the shore and then away from it again depending on several factors, such as the tides, the direction of the wind, wave action and the like. But the boat will never move further from the shore than the length of the rope. Now imagine that the boat symbolizes consciousness associated with the body/mind and that the shore symbolizes eternal, unchanging and unlimited consciousness. You need never be concerned, under any life situation, that you will be swept away from the Self as you are connected unbreakably to it. Ultimately speaking, of course, you are the immoveable shore itself. We are always that safe.

---

[1] Tolle, Eckhart (2005). *A New Earth: Awakening to Your Life's Purpose*; pp. 5-7.

[2] Peck, M. Scot (1978). *The Road Less Travelled.*

Chapter 26

BEFORE THE APPEARANCE OF THE UNIVERSE, I AM

In the 8th chapter of the biblical book of St. John, Jesus says, "Before Abraham was, I am." In this saying, we see clearly that Jesus did not take his body/mind appearance in time and space to represent his identity. Moreover, referring to the true Self most accurately requires the use of the present tense "I am" rather than a more grammatically correct "I was." Indeed, I *am*. I never *was*.

In the same vein, each of us can accurately say, as did Jesus, "Before the universe came into being, I am," as who each of us is – awareness – was present prior to the Big Bang event of 14.7 billion years ago which resulted in the appearance of the visible and knowable universe of forms of all types.

The universe could not have come into existence without there having been awareness present prior to it and out of which it emanated. So too, the universe continues to exist within, is witnessed by and is made of that same timeless and space less present awareness out of which it proceeded. In short, everything and everyone is ultimately consciousness. There is nothing other than consciousness that anyone or anything could be. Consciousness is the very ground of all existence.

And, once again, what is consciousness? It is the eternally changeless, irreducible essence of forms of all types. It has always been present. It had no beginning (as time itself is a form that has proceeded from out of consciousness). There was nothing prior to it. It has never not been. It will have no end. All proceeds from out of it. All occurs within it. All is made of it. How can the mind grasp this? It cannot.

Yet, impossible as this is for the mind to grasp, there is nothing other than consciousness. The universe is not conscious. Tom, conventionally understood, as we have seen, is not conscious. Other humans are not conscious. Only consciousness is conscious. Forms of all type are modulations of consciousness. Moreover, if I am conscious, then I must *be* consciousness. I am thus the only reality. Not, again, in the role of Tom. This is only an act, part of the play of the universe, a form of which consciousness is aware. But as the One conscious, aware Self. I am irreducible, eternal and timeless. There is nothing other than me.

I as consciousness am free now to know these truths knowingly. To embrace my true nature as being consciousness. To live based on this knowledge. What else do I need besides this? How does it feel to be finally liberated from the primary illusion that you are a separate self? You are free to answer these questions based on your own experience.

Moreover, "I" is simply the word we use to refer to the experience of being aware. Thus it is that I am awareness. Since awareness is universal and in fact pre-exists and contains the entire universe, then I must be universal and outside of both time and space. If I am that, then what are my problems? Ultimately speaking, there is nothing and no one other than myself and thus no problems.

John Greven expresses it this way:

What you are is nothing less than that which allows for everything to be. All appearance, whether it be a thought, a thing or creation itself is contained in and upon what you are. As with the Tao, you are the source from which all appearance derives, the un-produced producer of all that is, and the guarantor of its stability and regularity.[1]

---

[1] Greven, John (2005). *Oneness: The Destination You Never Left;* p. 46.

Chapter 27

God's Self and My Self are One and The Same

The astute reader has by now probably understood why I early on identified the words consciousness, awareness, the experience of knowing, the Self and other terms and phrases as being entirely synonymous. The term "God" is yet another of those synonymous terms.

This position is, of course, in tension with the perspectives on God of most believers, especially those associated with the Semitic religions of Judaism, Islam and Christianity. The conventional theologies which underpin these religions assume that God is a separate creator of all form who retains ontological distinction from the realm of creation. God is not, in other words, his creation.

Even the most philosophical varieties of these religions still posit a divine realm or intelligence which, though perhaps not quite a "supreme being" (as the more popular forms of western religion assume), is still other than the realm of form. Paul Tillich's "ground of being" and FSC Northrop's "undifferentiated aesthetic continuum" come to mind here.

The non-dual perspective, of course, eschews absolute separations, boundaries or distinctions and regards the world of form as emanating from out of the formless (or God). From this position, the realm of form (or "creation") proceeds from out of the formless, is underlain by the formless, occurs within it, is witnessed by the formless and is made of the formless. All form is thus, again, as Rupert Spira puts it, simply a "modulation of the ultimate formless."

Although to many people this understanding of God feels impersonal, it should be remembered that the synonymous terms formless, God, consciousness and awareness are also synonymous with love, peace, beauty and happiness. These words refer to the very nature of the divine. And the divine is unchangeable, eternal, outside of time and space and yet fully and always present in the eternal Now dimension. What's more, this is the dimension separation from which is impossible. "The Tao is that from which it is impossible to deviate," as it is sometimes put.

Could human life be more satisfying than being in conscious contact with this dimension? The obvious answer is "No, of course not." So why the enduring image of God literally as he was painted by Michelangelo on the ceiling of the Sistine Chapel? Consider the following explanation.

There is nothing prior to consciousness. Consciousness thus has no origin. It has never not been. How can the mind grasp this? Of course, it cannot. So, to defend itself against the implications of the above truth – the main one being that "I, as a separate self, do not exist" – the mind projects a creator God who then becomes the origin of everything. Ego, from this standpoint, is safe as the ultimate reality – or God – is understood to be an object which the ego self can relate to much as it would any other object. This abstraction then serves to preserve the illusion of ego as separate and real and thus represents a denial of death.

The entire universe as we have conventionally conceived of it is thus based upon a colossal hoax which consciousness has played on itself. The hoax is seen through as consciousness wakes up from the dream of form identity – that is, the illusion that my identity is limited to a human body/mind organism with a name and a history.

John Wheeler puts it this way:

> Just as the sky is never caught in the clouds so is awareness never confined or limited by the appearances in the mind. You are that awareness. That is ever-free. Ultimately you do not "get" free. You understand or recognize your ever-present freedom...Look and see if you are ever really apart from awareness. If you are not, then what do you have to do to become one with what you already are?[1]

This waking up process, as has been stated, continues indefinitely. Consciousness here and there, in this human and in that, wakes up. It is then that consciousness realizes that it has been operating upon a fictional basis – that of the separate self identity.

Consciousness further realizes that coming to the knowledge of the truth of my being is the ultimate purpose of this life. Questions such as "What is the remainder of this life for?" and "What am I to be about in this world now that the truth has been shown me?" can now be answered quite simply: "To know the truth. To live the truth." The fulfillment, joy and sense of realized purpose which then comes to accompany life proves that the Self is extraordinarily gracious, can be fully trusted and deserves our full commitment. The omega point has arrived at last.

---

[1] Wheeler, John (2004). *Shining in Plain View*; p. 77.

Chapter 28

I Am Awareness Itself

The undeniable fact that I am aware is, as implied above, much more significant than I had all along assumed. After all, awareness happening in the time and place known conventionally as Tom quite obviously strikes at the question of my very identity, which up until now has been hidden by the illusion of individual personhood.

The emergence of consciousness from the hypnotic trance of separate selfhood thus represents a profound shift in the One Self's understanding of itself. Now no longer viewing itself as sharing the limitations of the body/mind, it realizes its limitlessness outside of time, space and form. I am the One Self – once again, not as Tom, which is but a limited role I am playing or a character in the dream of the universal dreamer – but as pure awareness itself. Rupert Spira has called the above perspective the "consciousness only" paradigm.

Only God is Real

The main feature of the consciousness only paradigm is the claim that the limitless consciousness that I am is the one and only irreducible phenomenon – that which is indispensably needed for there to be anything else and which thus cannot be plausibly denied. Consciousness is, in other words, the changeless substratum underlying all form. All form is, according to this paradigm, made of, exists within and emanates from pure consciousness. "The Real is...the timeless, unconditioned, undifferentiated oneness of being," writes Elliot Deutsch.[2] Moreover, the Real is Brahman and Brahman, or God, cannot be known objectively but only in pure subjectivity.

Rene Guenon puts it this way:

> ...a distinct and definite knowledge is possible in respect to everything capable of becoming an object of knowledge. But it is not possible in the case of That which cannot become such an object. That is Brahma, for it is the Knower, and the Knower can know other things, but cannot make Itself the object of Its own knowledge, in the same way that fire can burn other things but cannot burn itself. Neither can it be said that Brahma is able to become an object of knowledge for anything other than Itself, since outside Itself there is nothing which can possess knowledge.[2]

What's more, the pure subjectivity of Brahma's knowledge of itself is available only in the dimension universally ignored by humans prior to awakening – the timeless Now. The Now. Simple, yet completely unavailable except by way of divine grace, election and unmerited gift. This is the key to the Kingdom of Heaven.

In conclusion, basing my understandings of God on the false premise of my own presumed separate selfhood leads inevitably to the projection of a God "out there" to correspond with the me "in here," both of which are understood to be objectively knowable. Thus it is that my seeing through the illusion of objectivity reveals my true identity to be identical to that of God. God and I are two terms that refer to the same phenomenon. For, as we have discussed earlier in this presentation, the awareness with which I am now aware, in its unlimited nature, *is* that which can be called God. I am that. There is no other. As the Sufi poet Rumi said: "When I sought God, I found only myself. When I sought myself, I found only God."

---

[1] Deutsch, Eliot (1969). *Advaita Vedanta: A Philosophical Reconstruction*; p. 19.

[2] Guenon, Rene (1945). *Man and His Becoming According to the Vedanta*; p. 114.

Chapter 29

TANTRA: THE SELF EMBRACING ITSELF

By now the reader has quite probably come to view from the "big picture," wide angle lens the aim of the One Self in the realm of form, which aim constitutes the ultimate purpose of the human species: For the Self to once again realize its identity as, and consciously re-unify itself with, itself. As we have seen, the Self that I am and always have been is the *same* awareness with which I have been aware all along. The astonishing realization that I have been observed all along by – and have been observing – nothing other than my very own Self implies a fundamental shift in my understanding of my identity. Witness and witnessed turn out, after all, to have been one all along. Two terms referring to the same phenomenon. The space of consciousness – the witness – and the apparent objects in that space – the witnessed – are both equally the One Self. Ego self – or the person apparently created by way of the Self's mis-identification of itself with the human body/mind – is, in fact, made of the awareness that is aware of it. Realization that inside and outside make up one field of unbroken consciousness thus eliminates the supposed need for separate selfhood. All form occurs within the undifferentiated field of consciousness. And I am all of it – "what there is and all that there is" – as Alan Watts used to say.

At this point, the Self comes to realize, in and by way of a human body/mind, that the circle which began with awareness apparently alienating itself from itself (the arrival in the Big Bang event of the realm of form), and which then eventually proceeded to its identification with the human organism, has now come back around to itself with the awakening of the Self to its ultimate identity.

While it is true that the drama of the Self's voluntary immersion into apparent duality continues by way of most humans, realization in a time and place – the reader of this book, for example – clarifies the ultimate meaning of the human drama and, indeed, existence itself as the process of the Self's expansion continues.

Here, then, is the prize for which all apparent ego selves are, however unconsciously, striving. Conscious re-unification of what, in truth, has never actually been separated brings with it the fullness and abundance of life about which Jesus spoke so frequently and with such authority in the New Testament.

Separation, alienation, materialism, duality, individual selfhood apart from the whole of the One Self, linear thinking, objectivity – these concepts come to be understood as, however temporarily necessary, relative, illusory and unreal. And what a relief this realization brings.

But, along with a sense of freedom and release, the Self's fully subjective realization of itself also tends to issue in a willingness to give of one's newly found abundance in an attitude toward the world of love and compassion.

Here, also, is the outward behavioral and attitudinal manifestation of the inward experience of liberation which makes up the Tantric aspect of awakening. The inclusive emphasis of Tantra* thus completes the depth-level and exclusionary aspect of the Self's Advaitic (non-dual) awakening, which is, as we have seen, characterized by the Self's dis-identification from the body, mind and world.

Dis-identification, of course, having been required by a new identification of consciousness with itself that cleanses or disentangles consciousness from all of which it has been conscious and in an unexamined identification with, is thus followed by a seeming "return" to the realm of form, but now knowingly both as its witness and the animating center of all form. The Advaita Vedanta emphasis and the Tantra emphasis are thus eventually seen as describing the truth from opposite positions and are entirely complementary with each other.

Tantric re-involvement in and with the formless is thus no longer based upon the Self's identification with the body/mind. And, with identity thus clarified, the personal projection and secondary identifications which inevitably follow upon this original dualism – self (the body/mind) vs. not self (everything and everyone which is not the body/mind) – fall away naturally.

---

* Tantra generally refers to the indivisibility of the Self and all form. It is thus often understood as the opposite of Advaita Vedanta, which emphasizes, as we have seen, the distinction between the Self and all form. Yet, the two emphases ultimately point to the same reality as the Self is non-dual and thus simultaneously distinct from and at the heart of all form. Historically, Tantric emphases are found in both Hinduism and Buddhism

For genuine and outgoing love is based upon the Self's identification with and as all form in a transpersonal embrace which knows no boundaries or limitations. This is the ultimate meaning of loving one's neighbor as oneself, as one's neighbor *is* oneself. There, in short, is nothing and no one that is not myself and, realizing this, I am empowered to serve others and the planet itself with an abandon and willingness born of the freedom from the bondage of ego.

Chapter 30

YOU ARE WHAT YOU ARE SEEKING

I recall a retreat at which a participant asked Rupert Spira what it was that he, the participant, was really looking for. Rupert replied: "The very awareness with which you are right now at this moment aware is what you are really looking for."

I vividly recall my own response to Rupert's answer to this question. "You mean it's that simple?! It's been here all along?! Right under my nose?! The awareness which is the knowing of all phenomena is looking for *itself*?! But it hasn't realized that and so has been looking in the realm of what it is aware *of* for happiness?!"

It all seemed, in a way, too simple. And yet, the simplicity is entirely missed and is made complex if consciousness, identified as this person or that, remains ignorant of its own distinctiveness from the forms of which it is conscious. And consciousness identified with most humans remains ignorant of this distinction.

Once, however, the distinction between awareness and the objects of awareness – thoughts, emotions, feelings, sensations, perceptions, images in the mind and the physical objects and people in the social and natural environment – is realized progress continues, usually over a lengthy period of time, toward a sustainable identification of awareness with itself in full subjectivity.

Here, then, is the new circuitry of awareness that is created when consciousness enters Phase One of the awakening process. The remainder of one's life then becomes, as Phases Two and Three unfold, a deepening of the establishment of awareness as awareness comes to know itself consciously and knowingly.

Moreover, far from having to accomplish this, we can leave this process entirely in the hands of awareness, as we have discussed. The limited ego self – Tom, in my case – plays no part. Tom, as we have seen, doesn't even exist except as a very convincing illusion. Awareness thus more and more comes to step out of its own way as it realizes its unlimited nature and the happiness and peace "which passes all understanding" (Philippians 4:7). What else do I need to know? I am it and that is that. To some, such as myself at first, this sounds too strange to be true. To others, it may not be satisfying enough to the mind. To others, eventually myself included, knowledge of this truth is like the relief a man who is thirsting to death feels when finally given water.

What's more, the process begins right here, right now. No preparation is necessary. The very experience of being aware is *it*. What could be simpler than the experience of being aware? Nothing. Everyone experiences it. It's easily the most self-evident and obvious fact of being human. Awareness cannot be denied, escaped, changed, destroyed or compromised in any way. The world cannot touch it. And so, if I come to realize that being aware of being aware is the experience for which I have always been searching, then what else do I need than the depth of the Now? What methods are necessary? How complex does this need to be? What do I have to do? What experts must I consult? Can't this be as simple as turning awareness to awareness? And isn't awareness always there to turn to?

Being aware of awareness, in fact, is so simple that it sometimes seems too obvious to talk about (though, of course, talk about it we must). How ironic that words show the highest level of limitation when used to describe the simplest of experiences. Awareness of awareness neutralizes all suffering, all illusion. It is the light that I am.

John Wheeler writes:

> You are timeless, ever-shining, presence-awareness. You can never lose it and never find it, because the one searching is that for which he is seeking.[1]

---

[1] Wheeler, John (2004). *Awakening to the Natural State*; p. 29.

Chapter 31

THE ETERNAL WITNESS

In our discussion of the sudden rising up of consciousness to the level at which it sees itself as distinct from the objects of consciousness – essentially the breaking into our lives of Phase One of the awakening process – we saw how consciousness comes to realize that it has always been witnessing the realm of objects from a changeless position outside of both time and space and that witnessing consciousness has never been in any sense either "contained" in human bodies or a property of the human brain.

In subsequent chapters, we then went on to consider the exploration of this apparently new dimension (Phase Two) and finally addressed the identification of consciousness fully with and as this dimension (Phase Three). We ended this aspect of our discussion with how Phase Three, in its emphasis upon identification, makes it clear that the Phase One separation of consciousness from the objects of which it is conscious is only apparent; in truth, consciousness is always only witnessing its own very self. In short, ultimately speaking, there is no difference between witnessing and the witnessed. These two apparently opposing poles are only linguistic terms for what is an ontologically inseparable phenomenon within which there are no boundaries.

As the process of the Self's awakening and transformation proceeds, it becomes obvious that the reality to which we refer and which we are cannot be captured in words and language, words and language being, of course, dualistic in nature. This, then, is the level at which both witness and witnessed are held together and within which both function – i.e. the true witness which we are but which cannot be witnessed because it is the very act of witnessing.

I am, therefore, what is both fully here and now, as noted in the previous chapter, and yet which is, *at the same time*, entirely inaccessible. Just as Adi Shankara in ancient times pointed out that fire can burn everything except itself, so I cannot witness the true witness that I am. I can, as we have learned, thus know myself only in pure and total subjectivity. This is the realm to which the mind cannot go, that reason is unable to reach. And yet, it is who I am. *Both* immediately present *and* unreachable at the same time.

Thus it is that all the great spiritual teachers have taught that mind cannot free us from mind. Fortunately, we come more and more to realize that neither does it need to. Liberation comes only from what lay deeper than mind and which is eternal and infinite. This is the "light behind consciousness" as John Wheeler has put it. When the light breaks through the darkness, therefore, it is not a supposed entity named Tom that makes that happen.

What's more, even perception is perceived. So that if one believes that she has reached the ultimate witness then one can be certain that this thought (as that is what the belief is) is also witnessed.

Witnessing is itself witnessed by pure consciousness, out of which the act is made and within which it occurs. It is the constant ever-present ground of being that alone makes sense perception, bodily sensation, thinking, feeling and imagining possible.

As noted in the previous chapter, the search is ended by none other than the searcher, who has come to realize it was searching for itself all along.

Chapter 32

I Am Free

We realize more and more, post-awakening, that, to the extent we resist our anxious, restless and discontent states of mind and try to replace them with happy states of mind, the more we remain unhappy and unfree. Then, as noted earlier, everyone and everything becomes either a threat I must defend against or an opportunity for ego enhancement. In this way I remain on the continuously turning wheel of karma, an ancient metaphor which refers to the self-reinforcing patterns of thinking, behaving and feeling that block true freedom, happiness and peace.

But to the extent that I am enabled to simply be the witness to my state of mind, to experience detachment from it, to that extent am I liberated in the Now and given victory over ego, karma and the shadow of unconsciousness.

When ego has thus lost its power to enslave me, there is no one and nothing that can move me, distract me or frighten me. I am aware of my ultimate trans-egoic, infinite and unchanging nature. Because I see all apparent events, things and separate selves as possessing as much reality as ego does - and that is, compared to the Self that I am, no reality at all - I am serene and non-reactive. This is the breakthrough to eternal life. "There is no self" said the Sufi mystic, Balyani, "other than the One Self. And no being other than the One Being"...

and "When you know yourself, your 'I'ness vanishes and you know that you and Allah are one and the same."

When ego is seen as both unnecessary and indeed fictional, then I am free to drop down below (or to rise above, if you prefer) ego. This "going below" ego happens by way of grace, which means it happens entirely by itself and of its own accord and not by way of egoic, or personal, effort. Efforts as we usually perceive them, after all, are too easily co-opted by ego as the acts, choices and decisions of an illusory and separate self. Free of ego, I am at peace and know the grace of God directly, powerfully and richly.

And when the need to concentrate, focus and act in the world arises, I use the capacities of the mind and body as needed. Without the encumbrance of the person, I as awareness am empowered to do so without hesitation.

Conclusion

We have, in this short book, covered a considerable amount of ground.

We began by asking the question "For what am I really seeking?" After identifying the seeker as not the separate self but as the One Self, we went on to address the question from several perspectives.

In so doing, we have insisted upon looking to our own personal and phenomenal experience, and not sacred writings, other persons or institutional leaders, doctrines or philosophies, as our primary source of authority. Indeed, it is in this way only that we come to *know* – and not simply believe in – the eternal, the infinite, the supreme, God.

So too, we have not flinched from the reality of suffering. Having removed it from the realm of speculation, we have accepted it as necessary at the level of dualistic experience. Indeed, as not only necessary but as even having the divine purpose of revealing to the Self, which we ultimately are, that we are not sufferers. We are instead that which witnesses and is aware of suffering, thus further revealing to us our supreme identity as awareness and not as victims.

So too, we have, stepping out of cultural conditioning, affirmed intuition as the highest level of knowing without degrading either reason or empiricism, the only two avenues of knowledge acquisition that are regarded as valid today. In fact, the entire presentation of this book assumes in the reader the capacity to "simply know" or "feel," by way of spirit, what is ultimately true.

Similarly, while we have made use of words, language, and ideas, we have been careful to avoid attempting a reduction of ultimate reality by way of words and language as they can only point to that dimension, not capture it. Once again, our journey through this book has been founded upon our experience and not the mind's formulations, however elegant they may be.

Following the establishment of the above basic principles, we have taken a close look at the human condition itself. In so doing, we have come to see that humans, in our being the One Self in the long process of awakening to itself, cannot escape desire, restlessness and discontent. So too, we have seen that for the Self to attempt a satisfaction of its search by way of ego is to further compound the issue. We cannot thus be free of the problem because all our attempts to be free *is* the problem. Liberation from the self-perpetuating cycle has thus represented a central theme of our discussion.

Further, spiritual liberation, when understood as that for which we are all primarily searching, however unconsciously, reveals to us our identity (which has been alternatively identified by using the synonymous words or phrases consciousness, awareness, God, the ground of existence, the One, the eternal, the supreme and the experience of being aware).

But to fully grasp the implications for ourselves of ultimate and supreme identity, we needed to examine more closely the phenomenon of liberation, which took the form of a suggested three-phase understanding of the process.

To briefly summarize those three stages: Phase One, roughly parallel with the purgation of the medieval mystics, is often called "awakening" by non-dual spiritual teachers. Awakening is sudden – sometimes dramatically so, sometimes so subtle as to be barely perceptible – in that it spontaneously "breaks into," as it were, conventional egoic, dualistic consciousness. The Self in Phase One has taken the initiative and has begun the de-centering of ego.

Phase Two, akin to the medieval mystics' "illumination," is referred to in this book as the exploration of new consciousness. This exploration, unlike the arrival of new consciousness, is not sudden but a process – a process which evolves naturally into Phase Three.

Termed "union" by the mystics of the Middle Ages, Phase Three is characterized by a gradual (in most cases) shift in identity from ego to spirit, from duality to non-duality, from person to God.

In their own ways, the three phases continue for the remainder of the human incarnation and thus should not be viewed as discrete, contained periods of duration following one another linearly. Considerable alternation among the three phases and their respective emphases can be expected indefinitely. Moreover, it should be recalled that, as Eckhart Tolle has estimated, about 15-20% of humans are currently the vessels of the Self in the process of awakening (have, in other words, entered Phase One); in most humans, the Self remains entirely identified with the body/mind. Finally, it was acknowledged that an entry of the Self into Phase One by way of a specific human does not itself imply that the themes of Phases Two and Three would necessarily arrive in that lifetime. It is therefore reasonable to speculate that other incarnations continue where the last ones left off (re-incarnations, that is, of the trends present by way of a previous incarnation, not the trans-migration of a separate entity).

Finally, we have discussed many of the gifts which come to us in the actual daily living of the truth of our essential beings – now identified more and more consciously and in pure subjectivity with the Self – as the result of ongoing transformation. This presentation was far from exhaustive and the reader could doubtlessly add much to it which I, the author, either did not address or did so only lightly.

My hope is that our discussion has promoted the transformation process that is taking place in you. For you are the Self and I have been speaking to none other than the Self. Indeed, there is no other. You have no need which is not provided for. All is essentially well and cannot – by God's will and grace – be otherwise.

You are free, without further preparation, to enjoy the Now. To go deeply into it. It is your birthright. Allow an immersion into the Deep Self. Into its peace, happiness, beauty and love. This is the Kingdom of Heaven, the dimension of pure awareness. It has always been, and will always be, who and what you are. The most real dimension of you. There is no need for anything else. There is no need for more.

Go with this truth. It is what you have always *really* wanted. Let the chips of life fall where they may. You cannot be harmed or separated from yourself and your essential identity cannot, under any circumstances, be changed.

And when the time comes for the body and all its stored memories to go in death, you will not be affected in the least.

Still

Time moves; I am still.

The body moves; I am still.

The mind moves; I am still.

She dies; I am still.

He dies; I am still.

I die; I am still.

Yes, still.

I still am.[1]

---

[1] Poem read by Kim Eng. May 2011 video presentation. Eckhart Tolle website.

Bibliography

Adyashanti (2008). *The End of Your World: Uncensored Straight Talk on the Nature of Enlightenment;* Sounds True, Boulder, CO.

Assagioli, Roberto (1993). *Transpersonal Development: The Dimension beyond Psychosynthesis*; Thorsons Publishing, San Francisco.

Balyani, Awhad al-din (2011). Know Yourself: An Explanation of the Oneness of Being; Beshara Publications, Cheltenham, U.K.

Benoit, Hubert (1990). *Zen and the Psychology of Transformation*; Inner Traditions Publishing; Rochester, VT.

Blake, William (2008). *The Complete Poetry and Prose of William Blake*; University of California Press, Berkeley, CA.

Borgeault, Cynthia (2003). *The Wisdom Way of Knowing: Reclaiming an Ancient Tradition to Awaken the Heart*; Jossey-Bass, San Francisco.

Bucke, Richard (2010). Cosmic Consciousness: A Study in the Evolution of the Human Mind; Martino Publishing, Mansfield Centre, CT.

Dante (2016). *The Divine Comedy*; Digireads.com Publishing.

De Shazer, Steve (1988). *Clues: Keys to Solution in Brief Therapy*; Norton and Company, NYC.

Deutsch, Eliot (1973). *Advaita Vedanta: A Philosophical Reconstruction*; University of Hawaii Press, Honolulu.

Dieckmann, Hans (1991). Methods in Analytical Psychology; Chiron Publications, Asheville, NC.

Eckhart, Meister (1981). *Meister Eckhart; The Essential Sermons, Commentaries, Treatises and Defense;* Paulist Press, Mahwah, NJ.

Emerson, Ralph Waldo (2019). *Self-Reliance*; Compass Circle (a division of Garcia and Kitzinger, Yanchep, Australia).

Eriugena, John Scotus (2000). *The Voice of the Eagle: The Heart of Celtic Christianity*; Lindisfarne Books, Great Barrington , MA.

Foster, Jeff (2007). *Beyond Awakening: The End of the Spiritual Search*; NonDuality Press, Salisbury, UK.

Gill, Nathan (2004). *Already Awake*; Non-Duality Press, Salisbury, United Kingdom.

Greven, John (2005). *Oneness: The Destination You Never Left*; NonDuality Press, Salisbury, UK.

Hartong, Leo (2007). *Awakening to the Dream: The Gift of Lucid Living*; NonDuality Press; Salisbury, UK.

Hawkins, David (2011). *Dissolving the Ego, Realizing the Self*; Hay House, London.

Heard, Gerald (1971). "Is Mysticism Escapism", in *Vedanta for the Western World*, edited by Christopher Isherwood; Vedanta Press, Hollywood, CA.

Hillman, James (1975). *Revisioning Psychology*; Harper and Row, NYC.

Hodgkinson, Brian (2006). *The Essence of Vedanta*; Chartwell Books, Edison, NJ.

Kelsey, Morton (1976). *The Other Side of Silence*; Paulist Press, Mahwah, NJ.

James, William (1958). *The Varieties of Religious Experience*; New American Library, NYC.

Jung, Carl (1958). *Psychology and Religion: West and East*; Pantheon, NYC.

Kant, Immanueal (2007). *Critique of Pure Reason*; Penguin Books, NYC.

Liquorman, Wayne (2004). *Never Mind: A Journey into Non-Duality*; Advaita Press, Redondo Beach, CA.

Maa, Amoda (2016). *Radical Awakening: Discovering the Radiance of Being in the Midst of Everyday Life;* Watkins, London.

Maharshi, Ramana (1988). *The Spiritual Teaching of Ramana Maharshi*; Shambhala Books, London and Boston.

McFague, Sallie (1982). *Metaphorical Theology: Models of God in Religious Language*; Fortress Press, Chicago.

Mooji (2016). *Vaster than the Sky, Greater than Space: What You are before You Became*; Sounds True, Boulder, CO.

Northrop, FSC (2013). *Science and First Principles*; Cambridge University Press, Cambridge.

Parsons, Tony (1995). *As It Is: The Open Secret to Living an Awakened Life*; Inner Directions Publishing, Carlsbad, CA.

Peck, Scott (1978). *The Road Less Travelled*; Touchstone Books, NYC.

Plotinus (1991). *The Enneads*; Penguin Books, London.

Rohr, Richard (2019). *The Universal Christ: How a Forgotten Reality Can Change Everything We See, Hope For, and Believe*; Penguin Books, NYC.

Rumi (2018). *The Book of Rumi: 105 Stories and Fables that Illumine, Delight and Inform*; Hampton Roads Publishing, Charlottesville, VA.

St. Augustine (2009). *The Confessions of St. Augustine*; Cassia Press, Santa Monica, CA.

St. Bernard of Clairvaux (2007). *Honey and Salt: Selected Spiritual Writings of St. Bernard of Clairvaux;* Random House, NYC.

St. John of the Cross (2017). The Collected Works of St. John of the Cross; ICS Publications, Washington DC.

Spira, Rupert (2011). *Presence: The Art of Peace and Happiness;* Non-Duality Press, Salisbury, United Kingdom.

Thoreau, Henry David (2009). *The Journal 1837-1861;* The New York Review of Books, NYC.

Tillich, Paul (1952). *The Courage to Be;* Yale University Press; New Haven, CT.

Tolle, Eckhart (2005). *A New Earth: Awakening to Your Life's Purpose;* Dutton Publishing, New York City.

Tolle, Eckhart (1999). The Power of Now: A Guide to Spiritual Enlightenment; Namaste Publishing, Canada.

Underhill, Evelyn (1955). *Mysticism;* Meridian Books, NYC.

Von Franz, Marie-Louise (1980). *Alchemy: An Introduction to the Symbolism and the Psychology;* Inner City Books, Toronto.

Watts, Alan (1972). *The Supreme Identity: An Essay on Oriental Metaphysic and the Christian Religion;* Random House, NYC.

Watts, Alan (1991). *Nature, Man and Woman;* Vintage Books, NYC.

Wheeler, John (2004). *Awakening to the Natural State;* Non-Duality Press, Salisbury, United Kingdom.

Wheeler, John (2005). *Shining in Plain View;* Non-Duality Press, Salisbury, United Kingdom.

Wilber, Ken (1981). *No Boundary: Eastern and Western Approaches to Person Growth;* Shambala Books, Boston.

About the Author

Transformation of consciousness began in Thomas Galten by way of recovery from alcoholism, a compulsive condition which Tom has since come to regard as a bellwether, as are all compulsions, for deep-level inner shifts.

Since the arrival of this new dimension of awareness, Tom has studied a wide variety of religions, psychologies and philosophies, research which has strongly influenced his practice of psychotherapy and teaching, professions for which he is formally trained and which he continues to practice.

But it is Tom's own inwardly experienced and ongoing renewal, begun in acute suffering and enriched by his exploration of the mysticism which appears in many settings, guises and disciplines, that continues to fascinate and engage him. It also inspires him to pass on to others, through both the written and spoken word, the esoteric knowledge that has been given to him.

Thomas Galten lives in Milwaukee with his wife and daughter.

Also from River Sanctuary Publishing

Enlightenment is Not An Ego Project, by Thomas Karl Galten. 2017. $12.95

The Ladder of Prayer: What A Course in Miracles Teaches About Prayer, by brother hermit. 2019. Hardcover $16.95

God Is: Ending Hell with a Course in Miracles, by brother hermit. 2017. $18.95

The Journey of One: a memoir of awakening, by Jenifer Marie. 2017 $14.95

Dreaming the Light, full color art and poetry, by Melanie Gendron. 2017. $14.95

Favorites

The Alchemy of Caregiving: Transforming Grief and Loss Into Wholeness, by Karen Young. 2012. $14.00

There's Only One of Us Here: A Guide for Aspiring Light-Seekers, by David DiPietro Weiss. 2012. $12.95

A Goddess Journal, (blank journal with illustrations and affirmations) by Melanie Gendron and Annie Elizabeth, 2015. $10.95

River Sanctuary Publishing
P.O. Box 1561
Felton, California 95018
www.riversanctuarypublishing.com
(831) 335-7283

We offer custom book design and production with worldwide availability through print-on-demand, with personalized service and author-favorable terms. Specializing in inspirational, spiritual and self-help books, biography, and memoirs, full color art books.

www.ingramcontent.com/pod-product-compliance
Lightning Source LLC
LaVergne TN
LVHW011419080426
835512LV00005B/153